William Westall, S. Stepniak

Russia under the Tzars

Vol. II

William Westall, S. Stepniak
Russia under the Tzars
Vol. II

ISBN/EAN: 9783337169916

Printed in Europe, USA, Canada, Australia, Japan

Cover: Foto ©ninafisch / pixelio.de

More available books at **www.hansebooks.com**

RUSSIA
UNDER THE TZARS.

BY

S. STEPNIAK,

AUTHOR OF "UNDERGROUND RUSSIA."

Translated by

WILLIAM WESTALL,

AUTHOR OF "RED RYVINGTON," ETC.

IN TWO VOLUMES.

VOL. II.

London:
WARD AND DOWNEY,
12, YORK STREET, COVENT GARDEN.
1885.

CONTENTS.

PART III. (*Continued*).

ADMINISTRATIVE EXILE.

CHAPTER XXIII.

LIFE IN EXILE 1

CHAPTER XXIV.

A DESTROYED GENERATION 54

PART IV.

THE CRUSADE AGAINST CULTURE.

CHAPTER XXV.

RUSSIAN UNIVERSITIES 73

CHAPTER XXVI.

SECONDARY EDUCATION 110

CHAPTER XXVII.

PRIMARY INSTRUCTION 129

CHAPTER XXVIII.

THE ZEMSTVO 159

CHAPTER XXIX.

THE DESPOTISM AND THE PRESS 187

CHAPTER XXX.

THE PRESS UNDER ALEXANDER II. 213

CHAPTER XXXI.

A SAMPLE FROM THE BULK 233

CHAPTER XXXII.

RUSSIA AND EUROPE 253

PART III. (*continued*).

ADMINISTRATIVE EXILE.

CHAPTER XXIII.

LIFE IN EXILE.

On an early June day, in the year 1879, all the exiles of Gorodishko, a wretched little town on the northern coast, are gathered near the landing-place. They number about thirty, and are of all sorts and conditions—young and old, vigorous and decrepit, some dressed like gentlemen, others like peasants, some in paletots, others in smock frocks, plaids, and jackets —pacing to and fro, leaning against the piles, sitting on bales of merchandise, standing in little groups and talking with the absent manner of men who are thinking of something else. From time to time they turn curious and eager eyes toward the upper reaches of the river. For it is thence will come the steamer, for whose arrival all are waiting.

There have been serious troubles at K——, a university town of Southern Russia. Beginning in the university itself, and arising, as usual, out of a misunderstanding with one of the professors, the disturbance speedily involved the entire city. A hundred of the students were expelled, and most of them—as also some others who, although they had been arrested, it was not considered expedient to keep in prison—were straightway ordered into exile. According to the accepted usage in such cases, they were divided into little groups, the leaders being sent to a dozen different places in Siberia, the less compromised to the northern littoral. One of these groups was coming to Gorodishko—an event on which our exiles were warmly congratulating each other. It was not, perhaps, very much to their credit to rejoice over the misfortunes of others, and the addition of six persons to thirty who were dying of *ennui* did not promise to be much of a distraction. But the lives of these thirty were so terribly dull that any event, however trifling, was regarded as a blessing. And the new arrivals came from without—" from liberty," as runs the mocking phrase, which sounds strangely in Russian lips. They bring with them a ripple of new life as a prison door, opening for a moment, lets in a breath of fresh air. So the exiles were gay, and prepared to give their new *confrères* a warm welcome.

They had long to wait, for in their eagerness the exiles had assembled on the wharf two hours before the time fixed for the steamer's arrival, and, as is generally the case in Russia, she was behind her time. But patience had become a habit with these involuntary waiters on providence, and it never occurred to them to murmur.

A young man from Odessa of the name of Ursitch, recently exiled for taking part in a " demonstration," had stationed himself, binocular in hand, on the top of a pile of wood. Every now and then those near him inquired if he could "see anything."

At length, towards three o'clock in the afternoon, he uttered the long-expected cry—" The steamer." And far away on the horizon could be seen a faint black line, surmounted by a thin grey column. A boat beyond question. But so small that a doubt arises whether it is *the* boat. May it not be some other steamer? The binocular is passed from hand to hand. Everybody stares with all his might into the double tube, but none can decide. The glass does not carry far enough.

"Uskimbai, the sultan!" shouts one of the exiles, "get up there quickly on the pile."

As if in answer to the summons a strange figure comes pushing through the crowd—large and solid—clad in a long yellow capot, with a deep yellow, hairless face, little Mongol eyes, a big flat nose, and a square neck, the latter covered with short black hair as crisp and bunchy as a horse's mane.

This was Uskimbai, the sultan—a veritable sultan, not merely so dubbed in sport or derision. For all the chiefs of the nomad Kirghis tribes under Russian domination bear this high-sounding designation. It is recognized by the Russian authorities, and after some dozen years' service these wandering sultans receive the commission of third lieutenant in the army of the Tzar. But instead of the insignificant epaulettes usually worn by officers of this rank, they are allowed to don the epaulettes of a major, the long tassels of which, when attached to the *khalate*—the sort of dressing-gown which constitutes their sole costume—have a remarkably brilliant effect. But Allah had not decreed that Uskimbai should receive this coveted mark of distinction. One night when he and some men of his tribe were quietly driving off a flock of sheep belonging to the garrison of a Russian post, they were caught by some Cossacks *in fragrante delicto*. The sultan, who fell into their hands, was taken in bonds to the nearest town, and exiled by administrative order to the northern provinces.

He moved with the rolling gait peculiar to men who have passed much of their lives at sea or on horseback.

"Get up and tell us what you see, sultan," said the owner of the binocular.

Uskimbai gave an affirmative nod, and did as he

was asked. He knew they could not do without him; a large smile broke his great beardless face in halves, exposing under the yellow skin two splendid rows of strong white teeth.

Pushing scornfully aside the glass tendered to him by Ursitch, and turning his eyes, or rather the two narrow slits in which a pair of brilliantly black cockchafers seemed to be hidden, towards the horizon, he declared, after a moment's earnest gaze, that the boat was the steamer. He said further that he could see three men on the bridge, one of whom wore a white hat, and was looking into a machine like that they had just offered him.

This seemed rather too much, and the declaration of the Kirghis chief was greeted with a shout of incredulous laughter, which evidently annoyed him.

"Thou Russian sees nothing; Kirghis sees everything. Thou'rt blind fowl," exclaimed the child of nature from his "coign of vantage" to the crowd below — "thouing" in the fashion of his country, whose language admits of using "thou" in the plural.

This sally was received with great good humour, and the sultan, descending from the timber with a dignified air, took a seat, singing the while a Kirghis song of triumph composed of only two notes, which he repeated continually in a slow and monotonous measure as if it were a funeral dirge.

Uskimbai's eyes had not deceived him, as fifteen minutes later everybody, with the help of the binocular, were able to see. The steamer was the steamer, and on the bridge stood the three men exactly as the sultan had described them. They were shortly afterwards joined by two others, whose costumes alone, even if they had not been accompanied by a brace of gendarmes, would have proclaimed their quality. When, doubling the wood-covered promontory which impeded the view, the steamer appeared in all her majestic grace, rushing with her black prow through the white foaming water, a great shout went up from the landing-stage, and the exiles made tumultuously for the gangway.

The passengers come ashore, and the new arrivals find themselves in the midst of a noisy excited crowd. Greetings are exchanged, and in a few minutes strangers and old stagers have made each other's acquaintance, and are on the footing of familiar friends. Three of the new comers are students, and as each in turn mentions the cause of his exile, the old stagers learn that the offence of their young comrades was putting their names to a petition. The other two are more advanced in years, and evidently not students. The first introduced himself as "Podkova Taras, advocate—for a shirt."

"How? You are indeed a cheap advocate to accept a shirt as retainer," laughed the others.

"No, no; I don't mean that. I mean that a shirt is the cause of my exile."

In this answer there lurked a touch of Ruthenian humour, for Podkova's supposed offence was Ukranian separatism, the evidence against him being, according to the statement of an informer, that he was in the habit of wearing the national shirt affected by the peasantry of his native province.

His companion, Dr. Michel Losinski, a professor of the healing art, was less fortunate. He had not been able to learn the cause of his exile.

"It was perhaps out of consideration for these gentlemen," he said, smiling and pointing to his companions. "The police did not think it right to let them make so long a journey without their own physician."

The introductions over and the formalities in the police office completed, the new comers were led by their new friends to one of the large communes, where a modest—a very modest—meal had been prepared in anticipation of their arrival. It consisted of fish, seasoned with powdered horseradish, specially brought from the dispensary of a monastery, six miles away, the sole possessor of this culinary treasure. For dessert they had a dish of carrots—

in that land of ice a rare gastronomic delicacy—the whole washed down with yellow water, dignified with the name of tea and drawn from a capacious samovar which seemed to contain an inexhaustible supply.

Conversation, the chief burden of it being naturally borne by the new comers, was kept up during the repast with great animation. The doctor was in vein. With characteristic Polish spirit (though born on the left bank of the Dnieper, and therefore "Russianized," he was a Pole by origin) he described the more comic incidents of his examination and preliminary detention, and told several racy anecdotes about the gendarmes of K—— and their proceedings generally. Orshine, one of the students, was called upon for a history of the troubles in which they had been implicated. Podkova spoke little. He had been a rising lawyer, of great ability and promise; but in the society of strangers his manner was timid and constrained. Orshine, who had made his acquaintance on the way, and was becoming warmly attached to him, said that Podkova, after one of his speeches, reminded him of a discharged electric needle.

The exiles did not separate until late in the evening. But as the new comers had neither told all their news nor exhausted their stock of suppositions, opinions, and conjectures, the divers communes, great and small, took possession of them as if they had been prisoners of war, and led them away. The distribution was, however, amicably arranged, and every commune had its man.

But what is a "commune" in this sense? the reader will ask.

It is a common institution of Russian university life. In all universities and superior schools a great part of the students form themselves into societies, each numbering from eight to twelve men, who hire rooms, make a common purse, and live together in full fraternity. In the common purse every man puts all that he receives from home, or earns by teaching, without thinking or knowing whether his comrades contribute more or less than himself. It is only by means of this system that so many poor scholars are enabled to study at the capital, and maintain themselves on their often very limited resources. But useful as is the system of mutual help to Russian students, to Russian exiles it is simply a matter of life and death. For without this sort of brotherly union and co-operation hundreds of exiles would every year perish of privation and want.

* * *

If the Russian Government were less besotted with fear it would surely let live in peace the suspects whom it sends to eat out their hearts in holes like Gorodishko.

Imagine a town "of about 1000 inhabitants," occupying from 150 to 200 houses, the latter in two rows parallel with the river and forming a single street. The spaces between the dwellings serve as short cuts to the forest and the river. All the buildings are of wood —except the church, which is of brick. If you ascend the steeple to take a survey of the country, you see on every side dense and wide-stretching pine-forests, broken in the neighbourhood of the river by great clearings covered with the blackened stumps of departed trees. If the time be winter, you have no need to mount so high; for you know beforehand that you will see only an immense ocean of snow, whose billowy surface is oftener traversed by hungry wolves than by Esquimaux sledges. In that inclement climate and almost polar region agriculture is out of the question. Bread is imported and therefore dear. The few inhabitants occupy themselves with fishing, hunting, and charcoal-burning. The forest and the river are the sole sources of their existence. Among the people of Gorodishko there are probably no more than a dozen who can read and write. These are the *tchinovniks*—Government officers—and even they are half peasants. Little time is given to bureaucratic formalities in this icy desert; and if you should happen to require the services of the chief magistrate, you would probably be told that he was away on a journey, engaged in the transport of merchandise, for the man acts as a common carrier. When he returns in two or three weeks and with his great fat fingers signs your papers, he will be happy, for a very moderate consideration, to drive you to your destination.

The intellectual horizon of these *tchinovniks* is not much wider than that of their peasant neighbours. No man of education and capacity could be persuaded to take service in so remote and wretched a place. They are either creatures without spirit or rogues sent thither by way of punishment; service in these regions being a sort of exile for the *tchinovniks* themselves. And if among the latter there chance to be some young *employé* ambitious of promotion, he is careful to avoid all contact with the exiles; for to be friendly with political pariahs would of a surety draw upon him the suspicions of his superiors, and probably ruin his prospects for life.

* * *

For ten or twelve days after their arrival the new comers had no fixed abode. The others wanted to make their acquaintance thoroughly—to know them —and they wanted to know the others. So they lived first in one commune and then in another, changing about as the fancy took them. After a while three of their number—Losinski, Taras, and Orshine—together with Ursitch, the Odessa man, formed themselves into a little commune of their own. They hired a small suite of rooms. Each member of the society acted in turn as cook, all their domestic work being, of course, done by themselves. The question of daily bread—naturally the first which presents itself—was their greatest difficulty. It was the means, too, of getting Taras into bad repute with the local police. The exiles brought, as they thought, enough money to last them until they should receive more. But the authorities did them an ill turn— made them pay out of their own pockets the travelling expenses of their escort to Gorodishko! And all their cash being in the hands of the chief gendarme, they were powerless to resist this curious and unexpected exaction. When Ursitch heard of the incident, he tried to console his newly made friends by telling them that the corps of cadets of which he had been a member were treated even worse. At the termination of the course, every graduate was made to contribute twenty-five roubles towards the expense of the canes consumed during their pupilage. But this anecdote, amusing though it was, did not seem to reconcile the victims to their loss. As for Taras, he was furious, swearing roundly that if he had known what the gendarmes were going to do, he would have thrown all his money into the sea rather than let them have it.

All were in great straits. Some even had not a sufficiency of clothing. People are arrested wherever they may happen to be—as likely as not in the street—thrown into prison, and in some instances sent away without being allowed time either to make provision for their journey or say farewell to their friends. This had happened to Taras. His fellow exiles placed their scanty purses at his disposal, but he refused to profit by their kindness.

"You have need of all your money for yourselves," he said. "The Government has brought me here by force, and deprived me of my means of living, and the Government must feed and clothe me—I will spare it nothing."

Not a day passed that he did not go to the office to ask for his eight roubles, always receiving the same stereotyped reply. The local authorities had written to headquarters, but the necessary authorization had not yet arrived. He must have patience. Nothing that he said or did seemed to produce any impression, and his companions asked him to desist from his labour in vain. He need not expect anything for several months to come, and to bother the officials would only set them against him.

"They shall pay me that money," was the only answer Taras vouchsafed to their kindly meant counsel.

One fine afternoon, when the other exiles were going out for their usual walk, Taras went out also, but so strangely dressed that all the children ran after him, and the place was quite in a commotion. He had nothing on but his night clothes, and a counterpane. Before he had marched up and down the single street half a dozen times, the *ispravnik* (to whom somebody had hurried with the news) appeared on the scene in a state of great excitement.

"Mr. Podkova, what on earth are you doing?" he said, in a tone of admonition. "Just think! an educated man like you making a public scandal. The ladies can see you from the windows!"

"That is not my fault. I have no clothes, and I cannot remain for ever within the four walls of my room. It might injure my health. I must take a walk occasionally."

And for a whole week he promenaded every day in precisely the same guise, paying no heed whatever to the *ispravnik's* remonstrances, until by his persistency he fairly vanquished official inertness and got his wretched stipendium. But from that moment he was looked upon as a "turbulent man."

* * *

The short summer, which in that far northern region lasts but two months, passed only too quickly. Autumn came and went almost unperceived, and then the long polar winter, with its interminable nights, reigned over the land. The sun, after showing himself for a brief space on the southern extremity of the horizon as a small arc of a few degrees of amplitude, went down into the long line of snow, leaving the earth in a night of some twenty hours, dimly lighted by the faint and distant reflections of the aurora borealis.

At this time, as may be supposed, the exiles of Gorodishko did not find life very amusing. Enforced idleness amid an environment destitute of everything that can fix the attention of a civilized man, must of necessity deaden the faculties and stupify the mind. In summer it is not quite so bad. There are berries and mushrooms to be gathered in the neighbouring woods, the authorities being good enough to wink at slight infractions of the regulation which forbids exiles to put a foot outside the boundaries of the town. A man can read, too, a resource which in winter is far from being always available. As candles are expensive and exiles poor, they can afford only rushlights made of fish's fat, or the *loutchina*, a splinter of resinous wood, whose flickering and uncertain light ruins the eyesight of those who use it for reading. For these unfortunates the winter, which lasts three quarters of the year, is a period of misery and inaction, a season accursed. The only way in which they can kill time is by exchanging visits among themselves—in the circumstances, however, a poor and altogether insufficient distraction. True, they are like a family. They would divide with each other their last crust of bread. But always the same faces—always the same talk—always the same subjects—their lives never presenting a new feature—and they end by having nothing to say. Men drag themselves first to one house and then to another, hoping that here or there they may find something less stale, flat, and unprofitable, only to go away disappointed, and repeat the experiment elsewhere with the same result. And this goes on for days, weeks, months.

One winter evening a company of exiles were gathered as usual round the samovar, sipping tea, yawning wearily, and staring at each other in dull silence. Everything—faces, positions, movements, even the room itself, half lighted by a single candle stuck in a big rustic chandelier of wood—bespoke the very extremity of weariness. From time to time somebody half unconsciously lets a word or two drop from his lips. A minute or two afterwards, when the speaker has forgotten what he said, there suddenly comes from a dark corner another word or two which, with some effort, the listeners understand to be an answer to the previous observation.

Taras does not speak at all. Stretched full length on a bench of pine wood, covered with dry moss, which serves both as bed and sofa, he smokes incessantly, watching with a dreamy air the little blue cloudlets of smoke as they hover over his head and lose themselves in the gloom, in seeming satisfaction with his occupation and his thoughts. Losinski is balancing himself on a chair hard by. Whatever may be the cause, whether worried by his friend's imperturbable phlegm, or rendered nervous by the electric influence of the aurora borealis, he is evidently more than usually hipped and unhappy. Though the evening differs in nothing from other evenings, it seems to him exceptionally unsupportable. All at once he breaks out.

"Gentlemen!" he exclaims, in an excited and energetic voice, which by its contrast with the languid tone most in vogue awakes immediate attention. "Gentlemen, the life we lead here is detestable! If we live on in this idle, purposeless way, a year or two longer we shall become incapable of serious work, utterly unnerved, and good for nothing at all. We must bestir ourselves, we must do something; if we do not, we shall grow so weary of this sordid, vegetating existence, that we may be tempted to drown our *ennui* and seek oblivion in the degrading bottle."

At these words the blood mounted hotly to the face of a man who sat opposite the speaker. They called him *Starik*, "the old one." He was the senior member, alike by his age and the greatness of his sufferings. He had been a journalist, and was banished in 1870 for some articles which had displeased people in high quarters. But this happened so long ago that the true cause of his exile had in all probability been forgotten even by himself. To the others it seemed as if Starik must have been born a political exile. Yet he lived in hope, looking always for some change in the higher spheres that might bring about an order for his liberation. But the order never came, and when he could bear the suspense no longer he would grow utterly desperate, and drink furiously for weeks, so that his friends were forced to effect a provisional cure by putting him under lock and key. After a bout of this sort he would quieten down, and for months together be as abstemious as an English teetotaler.

He lowered his head at the haphazard allusion made by the doctor, who continued to talk in the same strain. Then a shade of displeasure passed over his face as if he were vexed at being ashamed, and looking up he interrupted Losinski bluntly with this point blank question:

"What the devil would you have us do, then?"

For a moment Losinski was disconcerted. When he began his remarks he had nothing in his mind very definite or practical. He had started on the impulse of the moment, like a spurred horse. But his confusion endured only a moment. An emergency with him never failed to suggest an idea, and the very next instant he had conceived a happy thought.

"What would I have you do!" he repeated, in his ordinary manner. "Why, for instance, instead of sitting stupidly here catching flies, do we not go in for mutual instruction, or something of that sort? There are thirty-five of us. Every one knows something that the others don't know. Every one can give lessons in his own speciality turn and turn about. That will occupy the listeners, and stimulate the lesson-giver."

Here was at least something practical, and a discussion naturally followed. Starik observed that the sort of thing suggested would not be very amusing either, and that they would soon be more *ennuyé* than before. There were of course *pros* and *cons*, and the speakers grew so animated that they wasted their powder, several talking together, and nobody understanding what was said. The exiles had not spent so agreeable an evening for a long time. On the evening following the proposal was discussed by all the communes, and accepted with enthusiasm. A study plan was drawn up, and a week later Losinski opened the course with a brilliant lecture on physiology.

This promising enterprise was, however, of very short duration. The whole town was thrown into a ferment by the news of a proceeding at once so curious and so unprecedented. The *ispravnik* sent for Losinski, and gravely informed him that his lectures were in contravention of the regulation which expressly forbids exiles to engage in any sort of public teaching.

The doctor answered with a laugh, and tried to make the timid *tchinovnik* understand that the article in question did not apply to the exiles as amongst themselves. So long as they were allowed to meet and converse, it would be too absurd to forbid them to instruct each other. Though the point did not seem quite clear to the *ispravnik*, he was for once persuaded to listen to reason, or at least to act as if he did. He had fortunately as secretary a young fellow who, having almost completed a course at a gymnasium, was regarded by the people of Gorodishko as a prodigy of learning. It so happened, moreover, that the youth, having a brother in the " movement," was a secret sympathiser with the exiles, and always willing to do them a good turn whenever it lay in his power. He had already rendered them many services; but for reasons easily understood they seldom appealed to him. Such help as he gave was generally spontaneous. It was he who, in this instance, interceded on their behalf and decided the *isprarnik*, after some hesitation, to grant their request. But they little suspected that adverse influences were at work, and that danger threatened the project from another quarter.

* * *

The very same day, just when the shadows of night are beginning to descend on Gorodishko, that is to say, between two and three o'clock in the afternoon, a strange-looking figure walks rapidly down its single street towards a little grey house hard by the church, a figure covered entirely with hair. The lower limbs are hidden in huge and heavy boots of double fur—hairy within and hairy without—making the legs look like the forelegs of a bear. The body is enveloped in a *savok*, a sort of blouse or surplice, having long sleeves, and a hood, all of deerskin, with the hair outwards. The hands are lost in enormous *roukavitsi*, gloves of calf-skin—hoof-shaped sacks rather, because the hands would freeze in fingered gloves after the European fashion. As the temperature is forty degrees (centigrade) below zero, and there is a piercing north wind, the hood is lowered, completely hiding the face. So every part of the body—head, arms, and feet—is covered with red brown hair, and the figure is more like a wild animal which has learnt to walk on its hind legs than a human being. If it were to go on all fours the illusion would be complete. But as the figure is that of one of the most elegant of the Gorodishko beauties the suggestion is perhaps a little ungracious, if not positively ungallant. The lady is none other than the judge's wife, and she is just now bent on paying a visit to the *popadia*— the wife of the parson of the parish.

On reaching the little grey house, she enters the court and mounts quickly to the ante-chamber. Here she throws back her hood, showing a square face with large jaws, and eyes as clear and blue as those of the fish of the country, at the same time shaking herself energetically like a dog fresh out of the water, to get rid of the snow which has fallen on her furs. Then she enters the next room and finds the *popadia* at home, whereupon the visitor takes off her outer garments, and the friends embrace.

"Have you heard, mother, what the students are about?" says the judge's wife, excitedly.

In the far north political exiles are called "students" indiscriminately, albeit not more than a fourth of them are so.

"Oh, don't mention them! I fear so much that they will do me an ill turn, that every time I pass one of them in the street I make a sign of the cross under my *sarok*. Every time, I assure you. It is that alone which has so far kept me from harm."

"I fear now, though, it will protect you no longer."

"Oh, the very Holy Virgin! What do you mean by that? You make me tremble all over."

"Sit down, mother, and I will tell you. Matrena, the fish-wife, came to see me half an hour ago, and told me all about it. As you know, she lets them two rooms, and she has heard something through the key-hole. She did not understand everything—you know how stupid the woman is—but she understood enough to enable us to guess the rest."

Whereupon the judge's wife, with many exclamations, interruptions, and asides, repeated all the terrible things she had heard from the eaves-dropping fish-wife—and something more.

The students, according to this account, had conceived a diabolical project. They wanted to take possession of the town and everything it contained. "But as they are not allowed to do this they are angry. The doctor, that Pole, you know, is the ringleader. And, as you know, a Pole is capable of anything. He had the others in his room yesterday, and showed them things—such things! And he told them things—such things! It would make the very hair stand on your head to hear them."

"Oh, the saints of paradise! Tell me quickly or I shall die of fear!"

"He showed them — a skull — a dead man's skull!"

"Ah! ah!"

"And then he showed them a book full of red pictures, dreadful enough to dry up your bowels."

"Oh! oh! oh!"

"But, listen; there is something still more terrible. After showing them all these things, after speaking words that a Christian cannot repeat, the Pole said this: 'In seven days,' he said, 'we shall have another lesson; in seven days more another, and so on for seven times. And then, after the seventh lesson——'"

Here the speaker raised her voice, and paused for a moment to watch the effect of her words.

"Oh, oh!" exclaimed the *popadia*, "the powers of the holy cross protect us!"

"'After the seventh lesson,' said the Pole, 'we shall be strong and powerful, and able to blow up the city with all its inhabitants to the very last man.'"

"To the last man—oh!——"

And the *popadia* made as if she were going to

faint; but, remembering the imminence of the danger, she refrained.

"And the *ispravnik*, what does he say?"

"The *ispravnik* is an ass; or, perhaps, he has been won over by these plotters—sold himself to the Pole."

"Do you know what we must do, then, mother? We must go to Mrs. Captain. Come!"

"Yes, that is it. Let us go to Mrs. Captain."

Ten minutes later the two friends were in the street, both attired in the same grotesque costume, and if they had tumbled about among the snow they might easily have been mistaken for a couple of frolicsome young bears. But they were too much concerned about the fate of their native town to think of amusing themselves in this or in any other fashion. They hurried on to their friend to pour into her sympathetic ear the story of Matrena, the fish-wife, a story, we may be sure, not likely to lose anything in the telling.

"Mrs. Captain" was the wife of the captain of gendarmery, who had been a resident at Gorodishko for several years. So long as the exiles were few the *ispravnik* had been in sole charge. But when the number rose to twenty and went on increasing, it was thought necessary to provide him with a colleague in the person of a captain of gendarmery. The exiles were thus placed under the supervision of two rival authorities who were always on the watch to trip each other up, and, by a great show of zeal, ingratiate themselves with their superiors at the expense, it need hardly be said, of the luckless objects of their solicitude. Since the captain arrived at Gorodishko not one political exile had been released. If the *ispravnik* gave a good account of a man the captain gave him a bad one, whereas if the latter reported favourably of any one the former reported unfavourably.

It was the captain of gendarmery who on the present occasion checkmated his adversary. A well-drawn up denunciation was forwarded to the governor of the province by the first courier. The answer, the nature of which it was easy to foresee, was not long in coming. The *ispravnik* required a severe reprimand, and a threat of dismissal "for his careless supervision of the political exiles," and the license he had allowed them.

This rap on the knuckles so terrified the chief of police, that not alone were the exiles forbidden to give each other lessons, but placed under something like a state of siege. If there were too many of them in a room at the same time the police knocked at the window as a summons to disperse. They were also forbidden to form groups in the streets — in other words, to walk together—an order in a town of one street somewhat difficult of execution, and which led to several misunderstandings with the police.

* * *

Ties are easily formed in exile, for exiles, exposed as they are to vexations on every hand, to all sorts of annoyance and ill-will, naturally cling to each other and take refuge in their own little world. Like people in colleges, prisons, barracks, and on board ship, they are thrown so much together that the least similarity of character and sentiment leads to intimacies which may grow into lifelong friendships.

After the setting in of winter our friends' little commune received an accession in the person of the Starik, who had become much attached to them. They lived together like a family, but the two who seemed to form the strongest intimacy were Taras and young Orshine.

In the growth of friendships there is something strange and not easily definable. Perhaps it was the very contrast of their natures—the one concentrated and self-possessed, the other expansive and enthusiastic—which drew these men together; or perhaps it was the need of having somebody to support and protect that attracted the strong and energetic Taras to the frail boy, tender and impressionable as a woman. Be that as it may, they became almost inseparable. Yet when the others rallied Taras on their friendship he seemed annoyed, saying it was only habit, and in his manner with Orshine there was often a certain measure of reserve and restraint. They did not even "thou" each other, common as is this practice among young Russians. Nevertheless, Taras, while hiding his feelings under a variety of pretexts and subterfuges, watched over his friend with the solicitude of a devoted mother.

One day at the beginning of spring—in the monotony of exile, albeit the days drag as if they would go on for ever, the months pass quickly—the friends came in from a walk. They had been repeating for the thousandth time the same conjectures as to the probability of a speedy ending of their exile, and citing for the hundredth time the same signs in support of their hopes. They had also discussed, as usual, the expediency of trying to escape, and decided, as usual, in the negative. Neither of them at that time was bent on flight. They thought it better to wait. The revocation was sure to come. Both were Socialists, but Taras was all for influencing society largely, and in the mass. He was conscious of being an orator, loved his art, and had tasted the first-fruits of success. He had no wish to sacrifice the future of his dream—the only one to which he aspired—for the underground activity of a member of the Terrorist party. He resolved therefore still to wait, although his lot became ever harder to bear and patience less easy to practise. Orshine, on the other hand, had not a spark of personal ambition. It was a sentiment he could not even comprehend. The youth was a genuine type of a class of young men common in Russia, and known as *narodnik*— enthusiastic admirers of the peasantry. It had been his wish to leave the university and take the position of schoolmaster in some obscure village, and there pass his life, not in influencing the peasants (that would have been unwarrantable presumption), but in giving them the rudiments of culture. Though his plans were temporarily thwarted by the troubles at the university, in which he could not avoid taking part, and which had caused his exile to Gorodishko, he had not renounced them. He even desired to turn his enforced leisure to account by learning some handicraft which might help him to "simplify" himself, and enable him the better to study the peasantry whom, as yet, he knew only in the poems of Necrassoff.

When the friends reached the town it was already late, and the peasant fishermen were going out for their hard night's work. By the rosy light of the setting sun they could see a number of them preparing their nets.

One was singing.

"How these fellows work, and yet they sing!" said Orshine, pityingly.

Taras, turning his head, looked vaguely in the direction indicated.

"What a fine song!" went on Orshine. "It is as if something of the soul of the people vibrated in it. I find it very melodious, don't you?"

Taras shook his head and laughed lightly. But his attention had been roused, and when he came near the singer he listened. The words of the song struck him. It was evidently an old ballad, and he conceived on the instant an idea. He thought he had found an occupation which would help to while away the time. He would make a collection of popular songs and traditions, a collection which might possibly form a valuable contribution to folk-lore and literature. When he communicated his idea to Orshine, the latter found it splendid, another got the peasant to repeat his song, and made a note of it there and then.

They both went to bed in high spirits, and the next day Taras set out in search of the treasures which he proposed to gather. He did not think it necessary to make any secret of his intention. Twenty years before a company of exiles had openly undertaken a similar work, and enriched science with specimens of the folklore of Northern Russia previously unknown. But that was one time, this was another. The *ispravnik* had not forgotten the affair of the lessons. When he heard of the exile's new enterprise he was furious, and sent for Taras to his office, when a scene took place which the latter did not soon forget. The *ispravnik*, that brute with a thief's wages, dared to insult him, Taras ; dared to threaten him with a dungeon for " disturbing people's minds " —as if these stupid scandalmongers ever had any minds ! All the pride of his nature was thoroughly roused. He would have liked to knock the fellow down. But he refrained ; they would have shot him on the spot : that would have been too great a triumph for the blackguards. So Taras spoke never a word ; but when he left the police office, his deadly paleness showed how sharp had been the conflict, and how much it had cost him to keep his temper.

The same evening, when he and his friend were returning from a long and silent walk, Taras said suddenly :

" Why should we not go away ? The one can be no worse than the other."

Orshine made no reply. He could not as yet make up his mind. Taras understood. He understood also why Orshine demurred to his proposal ; for exiles, like long-married couples, know each other so well that answers are often unnecessary; they can divine their companions' thoughts and interpret their unspoken words.

The younger exile was in good spirits. A school had been opened at Gorodishko; a governess of the new style was on her way to take charge of it, and Orshine awaited her arrival with impatience. It pleased him to think that he would make her acquaintance, and take lessons from her in the art of teaching. He would have consented to stay a long time at Gorodishko if he might have had permission to help her. But of that there was no question.

At length the new teacher came. She had gone through a course of pedagogy, and was the first to begin the new system of teaching at Gorodishko. All the fashionable people of the place went to see the young woman at work with as much curiosity as if the school had been a menagerie and she a tamer of wild beasts. Orshine could not refrain from making her acquaintance, and when he waited on her he met with a very cordial reception. Passionately attached to her calling, the young teacher was delighted to meet with somebody who shared in her enthusiasm and sympathized with her views. Orshine left her house with a pile of pedagogic books under his arm, and his visit was followed by several others. But one day when he called he found the young woman in great trouble. She had been summarily dismissed from her situation "for having relations with political exiles."

Orshine was in despair. He protested energetically against the teacher's dismissal, and pleaded warmly in her favour, pointing out that it was he who had sought her acquaintance, not she who had sought his. But all was in vain; the authorities were not to be moved from their purpose, and the unfortunate teacher had to go.

As Taras and Orshine returned from the wharf, whither they had been to see her off, the former repeated the question he had put before:

"Well, don't you think I am right?" he said. "One can be no worse than the other."

"Yes, yes," answered the younger man passionately. He had borne the wrongs inflicted on himself with a patience and forbearance which to his friend was simply exasperating. But now the cup had run over.

"If we are not liberated this winter we will escape," resumed Taras. "What do you say?"

"Yes, yes; by all means."

The winter brought only new troubles.

* * *

It was mail day. Writing and receiving letters

were the only events that broke the sameness of that stagnant world. It might almost be said that the exiles lived only between one mail day and the other. The post arrived at Gorodishko every ten days—that is to say, about three times a month. Although, according to the regulations, an exile's letters are not of necessity censured, none of the Gorodishko exiles were spared the infliction, for the administration shrewdly calculated that the privilege of exemption, must be granted to all or none, as otherwise correspondence would be conducted through the privileged. They therefore granted it to none, and all the letters addressed to the exiles, after being read by the *ispravnik*, were resealed with his own seal and forwarded to their owners. Their friends never, of course, thought of writing to them anything of a compromising character, any more than if they had been actual prisoners, everybody being aware that all their letters passed through the hands of the police. But owing to the crass ignorance of the officials of that remote region, the censorship of correspondence gives rise to innumerable vexations. A scientific phrase, or a word of foreign origin, is enough to put them into a paroxysm of suspicion, and a long-looked-for and ardently desired letter is lost in the bottomless pit of the Third Section. The greater part of "misunderstandings" with the police are caused by the confiscation of correspondence. Letters written by the exiles of Gorodishko were treated in the same way. To prevent them from evading the humiliating obligation, a policeman was always stationed by the single letter-box the place possessed, and he seized without scruple any mail matter that an exile or his landlady attempted to post. A few copecks might have closed one of the fellow's eyes—perhaps both. But what would have been the use? The people of Gorodishko are so little given to correspondence, that the postmaster knows the handwriting of every one of them, and can recognize an exile's letter at a glance. Nor is this all. The correspondence of the natives is confined to Archangelsk, chief town of the province and headquarters of its trade. Letters addressed to Odessa, Kieff, Caucas, and other distant cities, belonged exclusively to the exiles.

To evade the censorship, then, it was necessary to hit on some special expedient, and it one day occurred to Orshine to utilize for this purpose a book he was returning to a comrade at K——. He wrote a long epistle on the margins, so arranging the book that, as he thought, it would not easily open at the parts where he had written. He had practised the stratagem before, and always with success. But this time an accident led to its discovery, and there was a terrible to do. It is hardly necessary to say that

Orshine had written nothing very particular or serious. What that is serious or particular has an exile to say? But Orshine, when he penned the epistle, being in a bantering vein, drew a picture more sarcastic than flattering of the fashionable and official world of Gorodishko, in which, as may be supposed, the *ispravnik* and his wife occupied a prominent place. The chief of police (who had discovered the secret of the book) was beside himself with rage. Running across to our friends' quarters, he threw himself among them like a bombshell.

"Mr. Orshine, put on your clothes at once. You must go to prison."

"Why, what has happened?" said the young man, in great surprise.

"You have been sending clandestine correspondence to the papers with the object of exposing the established authorities to ridicule and disrespect, and shaking the pillars of order."

On this the friends perceived what had come to pass, and were very much disposed to laugh in the *ispravnik's* face. But it was hardly a time for laughter. They had to protect their friend and assert their rights.

"Orshine shall not go to prison. You have no right to put him there," said Taras, firmly.

"I did not speak to you. Shut your mouth. Make haste, Orshine."

"We shall not let you take Orshine to prison," repeated Taras, looking the *ispravnik* full in the face.

He spoke resolutely and slowly, a sign with him of growing anger.

All took the same line, and thus followed a hot dispute. Meanwhile the other exiles, having got wind of what was going on, hurried to the spot and joined in the remonstrances of their friends. Taras took the lead, and despite Orshine's pressing and reiterated request that they would not compromise themselves on his account, they refused to let him go.

"If you put him in prison you must put us all there," they shouted.

"And then we will knock the old barrack in pieces about your ears," said Taras.

The affair began to look ugly, for the *ispravnik* threatened to call his men to arms and use force. In the end Orshine insisted on giving himself up, and his friends reluctantly allowed him to be taken away.

He was kept in the lock-up only two days, but the incident embittered still further the relations between the exiles and the police. The former took their revenge in the only way open to them. It so happened that the *ispravnik* had a morbid and almost superstitious dread of newspaper criticism. The exiles resolved to strike the man in his tenderest point. They wrote a sarcastic letter about him, and contrived to send it to a St. Petersburg paper by a roundabout way. The letter duly reached its destination and appeared in print, not only hitting its mark, but causing considerable excitement. The governor himself was annoyed, and ordered an inquiry. Many of the exiles and their lodgings were searched "for traces of the crime;" and as the guilty man could not be detected, all were suspected in turn, and submitted to every sort of petty persecution, especially as touching their correspondence. The police insisted on the strict observance of every article of the regulations, as to the application of which the exiles had hitherto succeeded in obtaining considerable indulgence. Losinski was the first to suffer from this change of policy. The eternal question of his medical practice again came up. A contention on this subject had been going on ever since the doctor's arrival at Gorodishko. The last pretext on which he had been refused permission to practise was that he might profit by it to make a political propaganda. Yet when one of the officials or some member of their families fell ill, he would often be called in. In this way his professional activity came to be half tolerated, without being officially recognized.

But he was now roundly informed by the *ispravnik* that if he did not strictly comply with the regulations his disobedience would be reported to the governor. The chief of police had no idea of risking the loss of his place in order " to give Dr. Losinski pleasure."

Nor were the others more tenderly dealt with. The supervision exercised over them by the police was almost past bearing. They were not allowed to extend their walks beyond the limits of the wretched little town which thus became practically their prison. They were continually annoyed by visits of inspection, equivalent to the roll-calls of the prisons. Not a morning passed that a policeman did not call to inquire about their health. Every other day they had to call at the police office and enter their names in a book kept for the purpose. Virtually they were in a gaol—a gaol without cells, yet surrounded by a vast desert which cut Gorodishko off from the world of the living more effectually than granite walls. The police, moreover, had the exiles continually in view; the latter could never appear in the street without being watched by one or more policemen. Whether they went in or out, whether they paid a visit or received a friend, they were always under the eye of the *ispravnik* or his agents.

This was all the more discouraging as there was little prospect of a change for the better. On the contrary, the chances were rather in favour of an aggravation than an amelioration of their lot, for, as they learnt from the *ispravnik's* secretary, a storm was brewing against them at Archangelsk. They were in bad odour with the governor, and it was probable that some of their number would be sent before long to a town still more to the north.

In these circumstances further hesitation would have been foolish, and Taras and Orshine informed their comrades of the commune, and afterwards the entire colony, that they had decided to attempt an escape. Their resolution met with general approval, and four of their fellow-exiles resolved to follow their example. But it being out of the question for six men to go away at once, it was arranged that they should leave two at a time. Taras and Orshine were to be the first pair, Losinski and Ursitch the next, while the third was to be composed of two of the older exiles. The colony talked of nothing else. The whole of the common fund was placed at the disposal of the fugitives, and to increase it by a few roubles the exiles imposed on themselves the greatest privations. The remainder of the winter passed in discussing the various projects suggested, and preparing for the great event.

* * *

In addition to the political exiles, Gorodishko possessed about twenty ordinary transports—pickpockets, petty forgers, larcenous *tchinovniks*, and other rogues of divers grades. These malefactors were all far more indulgently treated than the politicals. Their correspondence was not censured, and so long as they were occupied they were let alone. But they did not much care to be occupied, preferring rather to live by begging and pilfering. The authorities, who are "dogs and wolves" with the politicals, have great forbearance for the rogues, with whom they have evidently a fellow feeling, and take tithe of their plunder. These common transports are the scourge of the country. Sometimes they form themselves into organized gangs. There was one town, Shenkoursk, which they actually put in a state of siege. Nobody was allowed either to go out or come in without paying them black mail. At Kholmogori their conduct rose to such a height that the governor, Ignatieff, had to proceed to the place in person before they could be reduced to order. He called the rogues before him, and gave them a paternal lecture on their misconduct. They listened with the utmost respect, promised to behave better in the future, and, as they left the audience chamber, stole his samovar. As it was a very fine samovar, and the police were unable to recover it, a message of peace was sent to the thieves, and negotiations were opened for the return of the booty. In the end the governor ransomed his samovar with a payment of five roubles.

The relations between the two classes of exiles are somewhat peculiar. The rogues profess great respect for the politicals and render them many services—a respect, however, which does not prevent them from cheating their fellow-exiles and taking their money whenever opportunity offers.

As the thieves were less closely watched than the politicals, it occurred to Ursitch that they might be turned to good account in the matter of the contemplated escape. But though this plan had many advantages, it had one great drawback. The thieves, most of whom were confirmed drunkards, could not be trusted. Yet the co-operation of somebody outside their own body, if not absolutely necessary, was very desirable, and the question arose as to what they should do.

"I have it!" exclaimed Losinski one day. "I have spotted my man—Uskimbai!"

"The sultan?"

"Yes, the sultan. He is the very man!"

The doctor had cured him of an affection of the chest, to which the wild men of the steppes are always liable when transported to the frozen north, and from that moment Uskimbai had shown for his benefactor the blind affection of a dog for his master. He was a man upon whom they could count—honest and simple, a very child of nature.

The commune invited the sultan to tea, and explained what they desired him to do. He agreed without hesitation to everything they proposed, and entered heartily into the exiles' plans. Being under a much more liberal rule than the politicals, he was allowed to carry on a little trade in cattle, and from time to time visited the neighbouring villages, where he had several acquaintances, and would be able to conduct the fugitives to the first stage. In his anxiety to oblige the doctor and his friends, who alone at Gorodishko had befriended him, the poor fellow made little of the danger of detection.

It is unnecessary to dwell on the details of the escape. It was effected under the best auspices. Uskimbai acquitted himself of his task to admiration, and brought back the news of the fugitives' safe arrival at the first relay (stage) and their departure for Archangelsk. A week passed quietly; another an unwonted activity was observed among the police. It was a bad sign, and the exiles feared that some ill had befallen the fugitives. This foreboding was only too quickly realized. A few days later they heard from the *ispravnik's* secretary that at Archangelsk their friends had fallen under the suspicion of the police, and that, although they succeeded in getting away, they were followed, and after a chase of five days, during which they underwent terrible hardships, they fell, faint and exhausted with hunger and fatigue, into the hands of their enemies, who treated them with the utmost brutality. Orshine was struck and rendered almost insensible. Taras defended himself with his revolver, but was overpowered, disarmed, and fettered. The two were then thrust into a carriage and taken to Archangelsk, where Orshine had been placed in the hospital to be cured of his wounds.

This was a thunder-stroke for the exiles, and plunged them into the deepest distress. For a long while they remained in mournful silence, every man fearing to look his neighbour in the face lest he should see there the reflection of his own despair. And yet every object, every incident, recalled these unfortunate friends, whom a community of suffering had made as dear to them as their own kin. It was only when they were gone that they knew how much they had loved these lost ones.

On one of the three remaining members of the commune this new trouble had an unlooked-for effect. The evening of the third day after the arrival of the fatal news, Starik, who had been much depressed, was persuaded to make a visit to one of his old friends. He was expected back about eleven. Yet eleven came and went, and no Starik; but at the stroke of twelve the outer door opened, and the tread of halting footsteps was heard in the corridor. It could not be Starik; he was not wont to walk unsteadily. Ursitch went outside, holding a candle over his head, to see who the intruder was, and by its fitful light perceived the figure of a man leaning helplessly against the wall. It was Starik, blind drunk—the first time he had been in such a state since he had joined the commune. The others brought him in, and the work of looking after their unfortunate friend served in some measure to lighten the burden of their sorrow.

* * *

The year following was marked by many sorrowful incidents. Taras was tried for armed resistance to the police, and sentenced to hard labour for life. Orshine, before he had recovered from his hurts, was transported to an Esquimaux village in seventy degrees of north latitude, where the ground thaws only six weeks in the year. Losinski had a pathetic letter from him, full of sad forebodings. The poor follow was very ill. His chest, he said, was in such a state that he felt fit for nothing, "and you are not here to make it listen to reason." His teeth were playing him traitor, and showed a great desire to escape from his mouth. This was in allusion to the scurvy, a disease peculiarly fatal in polar regions. In the same hamlet with Orshine was another exile, sent thither, like himself, for attempting to escape. They were evidently very wretched, being often without either meat or bread. Orshine had abandoned all hope of ever again seeing his friends. Even if a chance of escaping were to present itself he could not profit thereby, so utter was his weakness. He concluded with these words: "This spring I hope to die." And he died before the time himself had fixed. About his death, moreover, there was something mysterious. It was never exactly known whether he died naturally, or shortened his sufferings by suicide.

In the meanwhile the lives of the exiles had become more and more insupportable.. After the attempted escape of the two friends the tyranny of their custodians increased, and their hope of being restored to liberty and civilization vanished almost to nothingness. For as the revolutionary movement extended, the severity of the Government towards those whom it retained in its power became greater; and as a further check on attempts to escape it was decreed that every such attempt should be punished by exile to Eastern Siberia.

But all the same, escapes continued to be attempted. The Gorodishko police, fatigued with their own zeal, had hardly begun to relax their precautions when Losinski and Ursitch made off. It was a desperate enterprise, for they were so ill supplied with money that success was almost out of the question. But Losinski could not wait. He was on the point of being transferred to another town because he had not been able to refuse the appeal of a mother to visit her sick child and of a husband to attend his fever-stricken wife. Fortune, moreover, did not favour them. They were compelled to separate on the way, and from that time forth Losinski was heard of no more. He disappeared without leaving a trace behind. His fate is therefore a matter of conjecture. Having to traverse the forests on foot, he probably lost his way, and either died of hunger or fell a prey to the wolves which infest that part of the country.

Ursitch, in the beginning, was more fortunate. Not having enough money to pay his way to St. Petersburg, he engaged himself at Vologda as a common labourer, and worked there until he had saved enough to continue his journey. But at the very moment he entered the train he was recognized and recaptured, and subsequently condemned to lifelong exile in the land of the wild Yakouts.

As he marched along the tear-bedewed road to Siberia, escorted by soldiers and surrounded by companions in misfortune, he met, not far from Krasnoiarsk, a post-carriage drawn by three horses and going full speed. The face of the principal occupant, a well-dressed man in a cocked hat, seemed familiar to him. He looked more attentively, and could hardly restrain a cry of joy as he recognized in the traveller his friend, Taras—Taras himself. He could not be mistaken. This time, at least, Taras had succeeded in escaping, and was now on his way to Russia as fast as three fleet horses could take him.

Quickly the carriage came on, passed like a flash, and disappeared in a cloud of dust. But in that brief moment—was it illusion or was it reality?—it seemed to him that he had caught his friend's eye, and that a gleam of recognition and pity swept over his energetic face.

And Ursitch, with beaming face and glowing eyes, looked after the fast-flying carriage, his whole soul concentrated in that last look. Like a whirlwind there passed before his mental vision all the sorrows which that face recalled, and loomed before him, like a vast gulf, the dark future which awaited his companions and himself; while he followed the vanishing form of his friend, wishing the brave, strong man every success, and making him in thought the bearer of his hopes and the avenger of his wrongs.

Whether Taras really recognized his friend in the fettered convict by the wayside we are unable to say. But we know that he faithfully accomplished the mission mutely confided to him. At St. Petersburg Taras joined the party of action, and for three years fought on—without resting either head or arm—wherever the battle was hottest. When at last he was taken and condemned to death, he could say proudly, and with all justice, that he had done his duty. But they did not hang him; his sentence was commuted to imprisonment for life, and he was left to perish in the Fortress of St. Peter and St. Paul.

Thus, at the end of five years, there remained of the little family by adoption, which had first met in that remote northern village, but one "living"—that is to say, free from chains. This solitary survivor was Starik. He is still in the same place, without hope and without future, not desiring even to quit the wretched town where he has stayed so long—for in the state to which he is reduced what is he fit for, the unfortunate?

* * *

My story is finished. Though it may not be cheerful or diverting, it has at least the merit of being true. I have simply tried to reproduce the reality. The scenes I have described are being continually repeated in Siberia and the northern towns, which the Government has transformed into veritable prisons. Even worse things than I have told come to pass; for I have narrated only ordinary cases, not wishing to take advantage of the right given me by the form I have adopted in this sketch to darken my colours for the sake of dramatic effect. To prove this I need only make a few extracts from the official report of a personage whom none certainly will accuse of exaggeration — General Baranoff, formerly prefect of St. Petersburg, now governor of Nijni-Novgorod, and who for a short time was governor of the province of Archangelsk. Let the reader himself read between the lines of this matter-of-fact document the tears, the sorrows, and the tragedies which so many of its pages reflect.

I translate, of course, literally, retaining the conventional expressions employed by a Russian functionary when addressing the cabinet of the Tzar.

"From the experience of past years, and my own personal observation," says the general, "I have arrived at the conclusion that administrative exile for political causes tends rather to exasperate a man and infect him with perverse ideas than to correct him (correction being the officially declared object of exile). The change from a life of ease to a life of privation, from life in the bosom of society to separation from all society, from a career more or less active to an enforced inaction—all this produces an effect so disastrous that often, especially of late—(observe!)—there have occurred among the exiles cases of madness, of suicide and attempted suicide. All this is but the direct result of the abnormal conditions of life under which exile places educated and intelligent men. We know no instances of a man exiled for motives based on serious suspicion of his political convictions leaving his exile reconciled with the Government, purged of his errors, and converted into a useful member of society and a faithful servant of the throne. On the contrary, we can affirm that very often a man sent into exile by misunderstanding—(observe again! what an exemplary confession is this!)—or by an error of the administration, becomes—partly owing to personal exasperation, partly by the influence of men really hostile to the Government — himself hostile to the Government. As for the man in whom are already implanted the germs of anti-governmental tendencies, exile, by the whole of its conditions, will favour the growth of these germs, sharpen his discontent, and transform his theoretic opposition into practical opposition; *i.e.*, into an opposition extremely dangerous. Among citizens who have no connection with revolution it developes, in consequence of the same conditions, revolutionary ideas, thus producing results diametrically opposed to those to obtain which exile was instituted. And whatever may be the outward conditions of an exile's life, exile itself gives the victim the idea of arbitrary administration, which alone is sufficient to exclude all possibility of reconciliation and amendment." *

The outspoken general is quite right. All who have succeeded in escaping from exile have almost, without exception, entered the ranks of the extreme Terrorist party. Administrative exile, as a correctional measure, is an absurdity. General Baranoff must be truly unsophisticated if he believes that the Government is not fully aware of this, or believes for a moment in the reformatory efficacy of the system. Administrative exile is at once a punishment and a formidable weapon of defence. Those who escape it become, it is true, determined enemies of the Government. But it is an open question whether this result would not equally come to pass if they were not exiled. There are numbers of revolutionists and Terrorists who have never undergone this ordeal. For every one who escapes from exile, moreover, there are a hundred who remain and perish irrevocably. Of the hundred

---

* *The Moscow Juridic Review.* October, 1883.

the great majority are entirely innocent; but ten or fifteen, or perhaps twenty-five, are really enemies of the Government, or likely in a short time to become so; and those of them who perish with the others are so many taken from the devil—so many foes the fewer.

The only practical conclusion Count Tolstoi could draw from the general's *naïf* report would be that a decree of exile should never be revoked; and this in effect is the principle on which the Government consistently acts.

CHAPTER XXIV.

A DESTROYED GENERATION.

So far we have restricted ourselves to a description of administrative exile in its mildest form, as it exists in the northern provinces of European Russia. We have said nothing of Siberian exile in general, of which the peculiarity consists in the senseless and despotic brutality of the least and lowest police functionaries, who have been made what they are by the system of penitential colonies which has prevailed in Siberia since its annexation to the empire of the Tzars.

In the latter part of the reign of Alexander II. there came into vogue another form of exile—that to Eastern Siberia. It still endures, and though considerations of space forbid us to treat the subject at length, is too important to be altogether ignored. The reader will remember that most of the men whose cases we have cited as examples of the extreme arbitrariness of the punishment of exile (Dr. Bely, Jujakoff, Kovalevski, and others), were banished to Eastern Siberia—the country of the Yakouts—a country apart, differing much more from the rest of Siberia than Siberia differs from European Russia.

We will not weary the reader with descriptions of this almost unknown land, but simply give the translation of an article which appeared in the *Zemstvo* of February 4, 1881. This article gives the substance of several letters on the subject published in various Russian papers during the brief period of liberalism which began with the dictatorship of Loris Melikoff.

"We know, and we are accustomed," runs the article in question, "to the hard conditions of administrative exile in European Russia, thanks to the bovine patience of our Russian people. But as to the conditions of Siberian exile beyond the Ural we have, until lately, known next to nothing. Our ignorance on this score arises from the fact that before 1878-79 instances of administrative exile in Siberia were extremely rare. In former times we were much more humane. The instinct of morality, not yet stifled by political passion, did not permit the sending of untried people by administrative order to a country in which exile is regarded by Russians as equivalent to penal servitude. But after a while the administration, stopping at nothing, began to banish men to places the very name of which excited horror. Even the wild country of the Yakouts is beginning to be peopled with exiles. It might be supposed that those who are sent thither are criminals of deepest dye. But so far the public has heard nothing of the nature of their offences, while, on the other hand, the Press has published communications which remain without contradiction, proving that these men have been exiled on grounds as strange as they are incomprehensible. Thus Mr. Vladimir Korolenko relates in the *Molva* his sad history, with the object, as he says, of ascertaining wherefore and for what cause he so narrowly escaped being exiled to the land of the Yakouts. In 1879 two searches were made in his lodgings absolutely without result. This, however, did not hinder him from being sent to the province of Viatka for reasons which he has been unable to discover. After passing five months in the town of Glasov, he was one day honoured with an unexpected visit from the *ispravnik*, who, after making a search of his lodgings without finding anything suspicious, informed our exile that he would be forthwith deported to the Huts (*pochinki*) of Beriosoff, a place altogether unsuited for a civilized being."

"After he had passed some time in these miserable Huts there suddenly arrived several gendarmes—

functionaries who had never been seen there before—
took Mr. Korolenko and his slender baggage, and
marched him off to Viatka. Here he was kept fifteen
days a prisoner without receiving any explanation, or
undergoing any examination, and then taken, under
escort, to the gaol of Vishne Volotchok, whence
there is only one road—that to Siberia. Fortunately
for him this gaol was visited during his detention by
a member of the Commission of Revision, Prince
Immeretenski, whom Mr. Korolenko prayed to inform
him whither, and for what crime, he was to be exiled.
The prince was complaisant and humane enough to
give him the particulars of the case set forth in the
official documents. According to these papers Mr.
Korolenko was to be deported into the country of the
Yakouts for attempting to escape, an offence which he
had never committed. The Commission of Revision
was just then inquiring into the system of political
exile, and a multitude of cases of revolting injustice
were brought to light. A happy change now took
place in the fate of Mr. Korolenko. At the Tomsk
étape (Western Siberia) he and several other unfortunates were informed that five of their number were
to be fully liberated, and five others sent to European
Russia. But all are not equally fortunate. There
are men who continue to enjoy the pleasures of life
in the polar circle, albeit the crimes imputed to them

differ in no essential respect from that imputed to
Mr. Korolenko. Thus the *Rousskia Vedomosti* gives
the history of a young man now at Verkoiansk, whose
adventures are truly remarkable. He was a student
at Kieff university. For complicity in some disorders
that took place there in April, 1878, he was exiled to
Novgorod, which, as being a not very remote province,
is reserved by the administration for persons whose
offences they regard as venial. Even the severe
administration of that period did not attribute to this
young man any political importance, as is proved by
the fact that a little later he was transferred from
Novgorod to the province of Kherson, which is much
warmer and better in every respect than the former
district. It is necessary to add, moreover, that,
according to the directions of Count Loris Melikoff,
all the students of Kieff university who were exiled
to towns in European Russia, for participation in
university disorders, have been liberated and allowed
to resume their studies. Yet one of these same
students is at present living in the Yakout country,
really because the higher administration thought fit to
ameliorate his lot by transferring him from Novgorod
to Kherson. The fact is that when Count Todleben,
the governor-general of Odessa, undertook to purge
the region under his charge of its noxious elements,
he exiled to Siberia, without exception, everybody

who was under the supervision of the police; and to this fate the *ci-devant* Kieff student had to submit, for no other reason than that it was his ill-fortune to be placed under supervision in the province of Kherson (forming part of the southern district) instead of that of Novgorod!"

"Another equally astounding instance of exile to Eastern Siberia is related by the *Moscow Telegraph*. According to the particulars set forth, this fate befell Mr. Borodine, a gentleman who had published in the St. Petersburg papers several articles on local economic questions. He lived at Viatka under police oversight. One evening at the theatre he had a dispute with the deputy *pristav* (officer of police), Mr. Filimonov, about a place, in the course of which the latter struck Mr. Borodine in the presence of several onlookers. The blow had a decisive influence on the fortunes not of the insulter, but of the insulted. Though the officer was not so much as reprimanded, Mr. Borodine was put in prison, and it required great efforts on his own part as well as on that of his friends to procure his liberation. His freedom, however, was of brief duration, for shortly thereafter he was sent by *étape* (that is to say, on foot, and with a gang of common malefactors) to Eastern Siberia."

"But how came it to pass that Mr. Borodine was exiled, seeing that his quarrel with the deputy *pristav* ended satisfactorily in his release from prison? We do not err in saying that the answer to this question is found in the communication addressed to the *Rousskia Vedomosti* on the exile to Viatka of the author of certain articles printed in the *Annals of the Country*, the *Russian Word*, and other periodicals. Yet his name was not mentioned. It was only said that while living at Viatka he committed, in the eyes of the local administration, a great crime. When the administration affirmed that the province was prosperous, he proved by facts and figures that, so far from this being the case, the people were dying of hunger. The consequence was, that this turbulent and disagreeable man—to the administration—had to submit to two police visitations; and at last they found among his papers the manuscript of an article intended for the Press — the supposed cause of the writer's exile to Eastern Siberia. After a long journey on foot, in the costume of a convict, with a yellow ace on his back, our author arrived at Irkoutsk. Here he had the pleasure of receiving the *Annals of the Country*, wherein was printed at length, without either abbreviations or omissions, the article to which his exile was ascribed."

"Let us see, now, what is the life of a man exiled in the country of the Yakouts. Here we have to notice, in the first place, the facilities for communication with the Central Government. If an exile living at Kolimsk should think fit to petition Count Loris Melikoff for a revocation of his exile, the petition would reach St. Petersburg in a year. Another year must pass before the Minister's inquiries touching the exile's conduct and political opinion can reach the local police. The third year will be taken up with the conveyance of the answer from Kolimsk to St. Petersburg to the effect, say, that the police see no objection to the petitioner's liberation. Finally, at the end of the fourth year, the Minister's order for the prisoner's release will reach Kolimsk. If the exile has no personal or hereditary property, and if before his banishment he lived by intellectual work, for which there is no demand in the Yakout country, he will risk death by famine at least four hundred times during the four years the post is making the four journeys between St. Petersburg and Kolimsk. The administration allows nobles by origin six roubles a month; while a *poud* (40 lbs.) of black bread costs at Verkhoiansk five to six roubles, and at Kolimsk nine roubles. If physical labour, hard and ungrateful to men of education, or the help of relatives and friends, or, lastly, alms given in the name of Christ, save the exile from death by hunger, the terrible polar cold will give him rheumatism for all his life, and if he has not strong lungs conduct him to the tomb. In such towns as Verkhoiansk and Kolimsk, the former of which has 224 inhabitants of both sexes, the latter a few more, there is no such thing as civilized society. Nearly all are Yakouts or Russian Yakouts. Yet the exile who is allowed to live in any town whatever may esteem himself fortunate. In the Yakout country there exists another sort of exile still more cruel and barbarous, an exile of which the Russian public has no idea, and is informed for the first time by the *Rousskia Vedomosti*. This is the exile by *oulousses*—that is to say, the placing of men administratively exiled one by one in Yakout *jourtes* (huts), distant from each other several kilometres. The correspondent of the *Rousskia Vedomosti* cites the letter of an exile living in one of these *oulousses*, which vividly describes the terrible position of an intelligent man thrown pitilessly into the hut of one of these northern savages."

"'The Cossacks who escorted me from Yakoutsk,' he writes, 'are gone, and I am left alone among the Yakouts, who know not a word of Russian. They watch me continually, fearing that if I go away they will be held responsible by the administration. If you leave the *jourta*—where you are suffocated—for a walk, the suspicious Yakout follows you. If you take an axe to cut some wood the timid Yakout tells you by signs to put it down and return to the *jourta*. You return and find sitting before the fire a stark-naked Yakout catching fleas—a fine tableau! During the winter the Yakouts live with their cattle, often not separated from them by the slightest partition. The accumulation of excreta of every sort inside the *jourta*, the phenomenal filth and dirt, rotting straw and noisome rags, the multitude of insects on the beds, the insupportable atmosphere, the impossibility of speaking a word in Russian—all this is truly enough to make a man crazy. And the food of these Yakouts it is almost impossible to touch. It is always very dirty, often putrifying, and without salt. If you are not used to food in this state it causes sickness and vomiting. The Yakouts do not know how to make either pottery or clothes. They have no baths, and during the long winter of eight months you become yourself as dirty as a Yakout. I cannot go away anywhere, much less to a town, the nearest of which is 120 miles distant. I live with the Yakouts, turn and turn about—six weeks in one hut, six weeks in another, and so on. I have nothing to read, neither papers nor books, and I know naught of what is going on in the world.'

"Further cruelty cannot go except by fastening a man to the tail of a wild horse and sending him in the steppe, or chaining him to a corpse and leaving him to his fate. It is hardly credible that without trial and by a simple administrative order a man can be subjected to sufferings which European civilization does not inflict on the worst of malefactors whose guilt has been pronounced by competent tribunals. Still more incredible seems the assurance of the *Rousskia Vedomosti's* correspondent, that even yet the lot of the exiles in the Yakout country has been in no way bettered, and that even recently there had arrived ten more administrative exiles, who for the most part are sent to the *oulousses*, and that further arrivals were shortly expected." *

One word as to the pretended incredulity of the writer of the foregoing article. It is a common subterfuge of the censured Russian Press to express thus, quietly and indirectly, its disapproval of the proceeding of Government. The *Zemstvo*, as every Russian who read the account knew, did not doubt for a moment either the reported arrival of the ten exiles in question, or the expected further arrival mentioned by the correspondent of the *Rousskia Vedomosti*.

We have thus reached the utmost limits of the official system of administrative exile as established in Russia. The *Zemstvo* was quite right—it is impos-

---

* This account of the conditions of exile among the Yakouts is strikingly confirmed by Mr. Melville's recently published book, *In the Lena Delta*.

sible to go further. After the facts I have exposed it is only figures that can speak. Let us then call figures in evidence.

The havoc wrought by administrative exile is far greater than that wrought by the tribunals. According to the particulars set forth in the almanac of the *Narodnaia Volia* for 1883, there took place between April, 1879, when Russia was put under martial law, and the death of Alexander (March, 1881), forty political prosecutions, the accused numbering 245 persons, of whom twenty-eight were acquitted and twenty-four sentenced to trifling punishments. But according to documents in my possession there were exiled to divers places—Eastern Siberia included — from the three satrapies of the south alone (Odessa, Kieff, and Kharkoff) 1767 persons.

The number of political prisoners sentenced in the 124 trials of the two reigns was 841, a good third of the penalties being little more than nominal. Official statistics relating to administrative exile are not procurable, but when, during the dictatorship of Loris Melikoff, the Government desired to refute the accusation of having exiled the half of Russia, it admitted that in various parts of the Empire there were 2873 exiles, all of whom, with the exception of 271,* were exiled in the short period between 1878

---

* See M. Leroy Beaulieu's work on Russia, vol. ii. pp. 445, 446.

and 1880. If we make no allowance for the natural reluctance of the Government to acknowledge the extent of its own shame, if we forget that, owing to the number of authorities who can issue decrees of administrative exile at their discretion without giving information to anybody, the Central Government itself does not know the number of its victims *—if, ignoring all this, we reckon these victims at about three thousand, the true number exiled in 1880, we should double this rate for the five years of relentless persecution which followed. In assuming that, during the two reigns, the totals range from six to eight thousand, we shall not be exceeding the reality. According to information received in the office of the *Narodnaia Volia*, Mr. Tichomiroff computed the number of arrests made to the beginning of 1883 at 8157, and in Russia arrests, nine times out of ten, are followed by exile, or worse.

But we need not dwell on the statistics of punishment. A thousand exiles more or less makes little difference. The great fact remains that in a country so poor in intellectual strength as Russia, all that is most noble, generous, and intelligent is buried with these six or eight thousand exiles. All her vital forces are in that great crowd, and if the number be

---

* See M. Leroy Beaulieu's work on Russia, vol. ii. pp. 445, 446.

not twelve or sixteen thousand, it is because the nation is unable to furnish so many.

The reader has seen what are the motives deemed by the Government sufficient to justify a man's exile. It is no exaggeration to say that spies and contributors to Mr. Katkoff's *Moscow Gazette* can alone count on immunity from this fate. To merit exile it is not necessary to be a revolutionist; it is sufficient not to approve fully and entirely the policy and proceedings of the Government. Under conditions such as these an honest and intellectual man is more likely to be exiled than to escape.

Exile in any of its forms—whether banishment among the Yakouts or exile in the northern provinces—means, with few exceptions, complete ruin to the victim and the utter destruction of his future. For a mature man, having some profession or occupation—a scientist or writer of reputation—exile is necessarily a great hardship, involving sacrifice of comfort, destruction of his home, and loss of work. Yet if he has energy and strength of character, and does not perish of drink or privation, he may possibly endure the infliction. But for a young man, who is generally a scholar, who has not yet acquired a profession, or reached the maturity of his powers, exile is simply fatal. Even if he do not perish physically, his moral ruin is inevitable, and the young alone form nine-tenths of our exiles, and are treated with the greatest rigour. As touching revocation, moreover, the Government is exceedingly stringent. Loris Melikoff's Commission of Revision granted only 174, and double that number were straightway sent to replace them. This fact is stated in the book of M. Leroy Beaulieu, "Much Ado About Nothing." And if among political exiles there be some who, after a few years' detention, are reprieved through a fortunate chance, or by the help of influential friends—without being obliged to purchase their liberty by the cowardly hypocrisy of a feigned repentance—suspicion pursues them from the very moment of their return to active life. On the least occasion they are struck once more—this time without hope of reprieve.

So many exiles, so many wasted lives.

The despotism of Nicolas crushed full-grown men. The despotism of the two Alexanders did not give them time to grow up. They threw themselves on immature generations, on the grass hardly out of the ground, to devour it in all its tenderness. To what other cause can we look for the desperate sterility of modern Russia in every branch of intellectual work? Our contemporary literature, it is true, boasts of great writers—geniuses even—worthy of the highest place in the most brilliant age of any country's literary development. But these are all men whose active work dates from the period of 1840. The romance writer, Leon Tolstoi, is fifty-eight; the satirist, Schedrin (Saltykoff), sixty-one; Gontcharoff, seventy-three; Tourgueneff and Dostorevsky, both recently deceased, were born in 1818. Even writers of minor talent, such as Ousnensky in *belles lettres*, Mikailovsky in criticism, belong to the generation which, beginning life in 1860, was far less harassed than its successors. The new generation produces nothing, absolutely nothing. Despotism has stricken with sterility the high hopes to which the splendid awakening of the first half of the century gave birth. Mediocrity reigns supreme.

Not one man of letters has shown himself a worthy inheritor of the traditions of our young and vigorous literature. As in letters, so in public life. All the leaders of our Zemstvo, modest as are their functions, belong to an older generation. The living forces of later generations have been buried by the Government in Siberian snows and Esquimaux villages. It is worse than the pest. A pest comes and goes; the Government has oppressed the country for twenty years, and may go on oppressing it for who knows how many years longer. The pest kills indiscriminately, but the present *régime* chooses its victims from the flower of the nation, taking all on whom depend its future and its glory. It is not a political party whom they crush, it is a nation of a hundred millions that they stifle.

This is what is done in Russia under the Tzars; this is the price at which the Government buys its miserable existence.

PART IV.

THE CRUSADE AGAINST CULTURE.

CHAPTER XXVI.

RUSSIAN UNIVERSITIES.

I.

At length we are out of the darkness and away from the abysmal depths in which despotism immures its countless victims. We have finished our excursions into that nether world where we heard at each step cries of despair and impotent rage—the death-rattle of the moribund, and the maniacal laugh of the insane. We are on the surface of the earth and in the full light of day. True, the things we have still to tell are not gay; the Russia of to-day is a very unhappy country, dear reader. But we have done with wasted lives and blood-curdling horrors. We are about to speak of the inanimate, of institutions which do not suffer, although they are falling in pieces. After crushing the living—the man, the artisan—the Government naturally and inevitably attacks the institutions which are the framework and support of human society.

We propose, then, to describe briefly the struggle of the Government with the most vital institutions of the country, institutions to which, because they favour the cultivation of the mind, it is instinctively hostile—the Schools, the Zemstvo, and the Press. The policy pursued by the autocracy towards these three cardinal elements of national well-being will show us what part it plays generally in the life of the State.

* * *

Russian universities occupy a position altogether peculiar and exceptional. In other countries universities are places of learning and nothing more. They are frequented by young men, all of whom, save the idle, are busied with their studies, and whose chief, if not the sole, desire is to pass their examinations and obtain a degree. Though they may take an interest in politics they are not politicians; and if they express sympathy with this or that idea, even albeit the idea be extreme, nobody is either surprised or alarmed, the fact being regarded as evidence of a healthy vitality, fraught with hope for the future of the nation.

In Russia it is altogether different. There the universities and the public schools are centres of the most intense and ardent political life, and in the higher spheres of the Imperial administration the name of student is identified, not with something young, noble, and aspiring, but with a dark and dangerous power inimical to the laws and institutions of the realm. And this impression is so far justified that, as recent political trials abundantly prove, the great majority of the young men who throw themselves into the struggle for liberty are under thirty, and belong either to the class of undergraduates or to those whose academic honours are newly won. This, though it may surprise Englishmen, is neither unprecedented nor unnatural. When a government in possession of despotic power punishes as a crime the least show of opposition to its will, nearly all whom age has made cautious or wealth selfish, or who have given hostages to fortunes, shun the strife. It is then that the leaders of the forlorn hope turn to the young, who, though they may lack knowledge and experience, are rarely wanting either in courage or devotion. It was thus in Italy at the time of the Mazzinian conspiracies; in Spain at the time of Riego and Queroga; in Germany at the time of the Tugenbund, and again about the middle of this century. If the transfer of the centre of political gravity to the young is more marked in Russia than it has been elsewhere, it is that the determining causes have been more powerful in their action and more prolonged in their duration. One of the most potent of these causes is the conduct of the Government, whose ill-judged measures of repression exasperate the youth of our universities and convert latent discontent into flat rebellion. That this is no mere assertion, the facts I am about to adduce will sufficiently prove.

Towards the end of 1878 there occurred among the students of St. Petersburg university some so-called "disorders." They were not serious, and in ordinary circumstances would have been punished by sending a few score young fellows to waste the rest of their lives in some obscure village of the far north, and neither the Ministry nor the University Council would have given the matter further thought. But this time there was a new departure. After passing judgment on the rioters, the Council appointed a commission of twelve, among whom were some of the best professors of the university, to institute a searching inquiry into the cause of these troubles, which recur with periodical regularity. After discussing the question at length, the Commission prepared a draft petition for presentation to the Emperor, demanding his sanction for a thorough reform of the disciplinary regulations of the university. This proposal did not, however, find favour with the Council;

instead of it they drew up a report to the Ministry " on the causes of the disorders and the best means of preventing a renewal thereof."

The document, which is of the highest interest, was published neither in the annual report of the university nor by the Press. Any journal which had dared even to refer to it would have been promptly suspended. But a few copies were printed in the clandestine office of the *Zemlya a Volia*, and those of them that still exist are prized as rare bibliographic curiosities. From a copy in my possession I make the following extracts, which, as will be seen, give a vivid description of the rule under which the students are compelled to live, and the irritating treatment to which they are expected to submit:—

"Of all departments of the administration the one with which students come most in contact is the Department of Police. By its proceedings they naturally form their opinion of the character of the Government. It is, therefore, in their interest, and that of the State, that the conduct of the police towards the members of our universities should be kind, considerate, and reasonable. But it is precisely the reverse. For most young men intercourse with comrades and friends is an absolute necessity. To satisfy this necessity there exists in all other European universities (as also in those of

Finland and the Baltic provinces, which enjoy considerable local liberties) special institutions, such as clubs, corporations, and unions. At St. Petersburg there is nothing of the sort, although the great majority of the students, being from the country, have no friends in the city with whom they can associate. Private reunions might, in some measure, make up for deprivation of other opportunities of social intercourse were it not that police interference renders the one almost as impossible as the other. A meeting of several students in the room of one of their number draws immediate attention and gives rise to exaggerated fears. The porters, and even the proprietors of the rooms, are bound on their peril to give prompt information of the fact to the police, by whom such meetings are often dispersed. Besides being practically forbidden to enjoy each other's society, students, even in the privacy of their own chambers, are not free from annoyance. Although they may lead studious lives, meddle with nobody, and receive and make few visits, they are none the less submitted to a rigorous oversight." (The professors observe, not without malice, that *everybody* is under police supervision. Everything, however, depends on the form it takes and the extent to which it is exercised ; and the supervision exercised over the students, ceasing to be a measure of public security, became an interference with their private life.)

"'How does he pass his time?' 'Whom does he associate with?' 'What time does he generally come home?' 'What does he read?' 'What does he write?' are among the questions put by the police to porters and lodging-house keepers, people generally of little or no education, who carry out their instructions with scant regard for the feelings of impressionable youth." (Read between the lines this means that during the absence of the students their books and papers are overhauled, and anything in them that may appear suspicious brought under the notice of the police.)

This is the testimony of the heads of the University of St. Petersburg, speaking in confidence to the Ministers of the Tzar.* But these worthy gentlemen

---

* Shortly after the appearance of the article which forms the substance of this chapter in the *Times*, Mr. Katkoff, in a warm and eloquent leader in the *Moscow Gazette*, roundly accused me of having invented both the commission of professors and their report; neither of which, according to him, ever existed. As the facts are rather of old date and almost forgotten by the public, and as the charge may be repeated, I am constrained, in my own justification, to mention certain details and to give the names which, in the first instance, I omitted. The commission nominated by the University is no more a myth than the twelve professors of whom it was composed, and who took part in its proceedings. MM. Beketoff, Faminzine, Butleroff, Setchenoff, Gradovsky, Serguevitch, Taganzeff, Vladislavleff, Miller, Laman-

told only half the truth. Their remarks apply solely to the treatment of students outside the university. A natural feeling of delicacy restrained them from dwelling on the things that are done within the walls, where learning and science should reign supreme. The interior oversight of the undergraduate is entrusted to a so-called "Inspection," composed of an inspector, appointed by the Ministry, several sub-inspectors, and a number of agents. The students, like the professors, live outside the precincts of the University and meet in the *aulas* only at appointed hours, and for the sole object of attending the lectures that are there given. The professors are quite competent to maintain order in the schools.

And what good purpose can be served by submitting this noble and pacific activity to special police oversight? As well organize a special force of spurred and helmeted sacristans to supervise the faithful when they meet for Divine worship. In Russia, however, it is precisely because universities are laboratories of thought and ideas in constant action, that their supervision is deemed, above all things, desirable ; and that inspection of their do-

---

sky, Khoolson, and Gotstunsky. I hope these gentlemen, most of whom are still professors in St. Petersburg University, are in good health. Their report was drawn up on December 14, 1878. It is not very long since. They doubtless remember the circumstance, and the question can easily be put.

mestic life is the point kept most in view. Having nothing to do with study, being in no wise subject either to the management or to the University Council, depending only on the high police, and the Ministry, this heterogeneous element, like a foreign substance introduced into a living body, deranges all the natural functions of a scholastic institution.

Three-fourths of the so-called "university disorders" are caused by the meddlings of the divers agents of the inspection. The inspector—and herein lies the chief cause of the universal detestation in which he is held—is a delegate of the general police; an Argus sent into the enemy's camp to detect the seeds of sedition. A word whispered in the ear may entail consequences the reverse of agreeable, not alone on an unfortunate student but on a college don of high rank.

These hated spies, moreover, enjoy the most extensive powers. An inspector can do almost anything. With the approbation of the curator, that is to say, of the Minister who directs his proceedings, he may expel a student for one or two years, or for ever, without any sort of inquiry or trial. The same functionary controls the scholarships and bursaries, so numerous in Russian superior schools, and by his mere veto can deny them to the destined recipients by classing the latter as *neblagonadejen*—a word for which the English language has no equivalent, meaning that, albeit the victims are not yet under suspicion they cannot be regarded as altogether impeccable. The inspector wields yet another power. By a stroke of the pen he can deprive a host of students of the means of livelihood in forbidding them to give private lessons. Many of the students being very poor, are dependent on work of this sort for their daily bread. No one can give private lessons without police authorization, and authorization is never given without the approval of the inspector, and then only for a limited time. The inspector may, at his own good pleasure, prevent the renewal of the authorization, or even cancel it before the expiration of the term for which it was granted. This officer, and each of his agents, is also empowered to punish refractory students by imprisonment in a dungeon for any time not exceeding seven days. He may reprimand them for coming late to lecture, for wearing clothes he does not like, for the cut of their hair and the cock of their hats, and otherwise torment them with any puerilities it may please him to inflict.

II.

These petty tyrannies are, if possible, more keenly felt and more bitterly resented by Russian students than they would be by students of other nationalities. Our young men are precocious. The sufferings they witness and the persecutions they endure bring them rapidly to maturity. A Russian student unites the dignity of manhood with the ardour of youth, and feels the outrages to which he is exposed all the more acutely that he is powerless to resist them. The students belong for the most part to the lower nobility and the lower clergy, both of whom are poor. All are familiar with the literature of Liberalism and free-thought, and the great majority are imbued with democratic and anti-despotic ideas. As they grow older these ideas become intensified by the conditions under which they live. They are compelled either to serve a Government which they detest or betake themselves to callings for which they may have little aptitude. Russia has absolutely no future for young men of noble natures and generous aspiration. Unless they consent to don the livery of the Tzar, or become members of a corrupt bureaucracy, they can neither serve their country nor take part in public affairs. In these circumstances it is no wonder that seditious notions are rampant among the students of Russian universities, and that they should ever be ready to take part in demonstrations against authority in general, and, above all, against their enemies of the police—demonstrations which in official phraseology become "disorders" and "troubles," and are ascribed to the machinations of the revolutionary party. The charge is false. The revolutionary party gains nothing by this warfare. On the contrary, they are weakened; because those who are lost to the cause through a university squabble might have used their energies to better purpose in a truly revolutionary struggle. The disorders in our universities are entirely spontaneous; they have no other cause than latent discontent, which, always accumulating, is ever ready to vent itself in a "manifestation." A student is unjustly expelled from the university; another is arbitrarily deprived of his bursary; an unpopular professor requests the inspectors to force undergraduates into his lecture-room. The news spreads, the students are excited, they gather in twos and threes to discuss the matter, and, finally, a general meeting is called to protest against the action of the authorities, and demand reparation for the injustice they have committed. The rector appears and declines to make any explanation; the inspector orders the meeting to disperse forthwith. The students, now in a white heat of indignation, refuse to obey; whereupon the inspector, who had anticipated this contingency, calls into the room a force of gendarmes, Cossacks, and soldiers, and the meeting is dissolved by main force.

An incident that occurred at Moscow in December, 1880, affords an apt illustration of the trivial causes from which disorders sometimes arise. Professor Zernoff was giving a lecture on anatomy to an attentive audience, when a loud and unusual noise being heard in the next room, most of the students ran out to see what had happened. Nothing particular had happened, but the professor, annoyed by the interruption of his lecture, made a complaint to the authorities. The next day it was stated that the complaint had led to the expulsion of several members of the class. A punishment so severe for an offence so venial kindled general indignation. A meeting was called and a resolution passed calling upon the rector for an explanation. But instead of the rector came the chief of the Moscow police, followed by a great array of gendarmes, Cossacks, and infantry, who ordered the meeting to disperse. The young fellows were now greatly excited and, though they would have listened to reason, refused obedience to the behests of brute force. On this the *aula* was surrounded by the soldiers, all the issues were beset, the students, to the number of four hundred were taken prisoners, and amid a square of bayonets marched off to gaol.

Affairs of this sort do not always end with simple arrests. At the least show of resistance the foot soldiers make free use of the butt-ends of their muskets, the Cossacks ply their whips, the faces of the students stream with blood, some are thrown wounded to the ground, and there ensues a terrible scene of armed violence and unavailing resistance. It happened thus at Kharkoff, in November, 1878, when some troubles arose from a mere misunderstanding between a professor at the Veterinary College and one of his classes—a misunderstanding which a few words of explanation would have sufficed to remove. It was thus at Moscow and St. Petersburg during the disorders of 1861, 1863, and 1866; and in certain circumstances the law sanctions even grosser outrages. In 1878 an enactment, the cruelty of which it is impossible to exaggerate, was promulgated. "Considering," it ran, "the frequency of students' meetings in the universities and public schools, the law concerning seditious gatherings in the streets and other public places is applied to all buildings and establishments used as colleges and superior schools." Thus all students in Russia are placed permanently under martial law. A meeting or group of undergraduates, after being summoned three times to disperse, may be shot down as if they were armed rebels.

Happily, however, this monstrous law has not yet been applied in all its rigour. The police still limit their repressive measures to beating and imprisoning the students who contravene their commands or otherwise incur their displeasure. But the students, so far from being grateful for this moderation, are always in a state of simmering revolt, and lose no opportunity of protesting, by deed and word, against the tyrannical proceedings of the agents of the law. There is, moreover, a strong fellow-feeling among them, and "disorders" at one university are often a signal for disorders at half a dozen other seats of learning. The troubles which began at the end of 1882 extended over nearly the whole of scholastic Russia. They began in the far east, at the University of Kazan. Firsoff, the rector, deprived a young man named Voronzoff of his bursary, a thing which he had no right to do, the bursary having been granted by the Zemstvo of Voronzoff's native province. Voronzoff was so exasperated that he publicly boxed the rector's ears. In ordinary circumstances, and in a well-ordered university, an outrage so gross would have provoked general indignation, and the students themselves would have stigmatized the offence as it deserved. But the rector's despotic rule had rendered him so unpopular that on the day of Voronzoff's expulsion the students—some six hundred in number—broke open the assembly room, and held a tumultuous meeting, whereupon Pro-rector Voulitch hurried to the spot and ordered the assembly to disperse. Nobody listened to him. Two of the students made speeches against Firsoff and defended Voronzoff. A former student of Moscow university, without giving heed to the presence of Voulitch, spoke in the most violent terms against the curator, the rector, and the professors generally. In the end the meeting voted and presented to Pro-rector Voulitch a petition demanding Rector Firsoff's immediate dismissal, and the revocation of Voronzoff's expulsion.

Then, before dispersing, the students resolved to meet again on the following day. On this the heads of the university applied to the governor of the province for the means of restoring order, and the great man promptly placed at their disposal several companies of infantry and a large force of police. A few days later it was announced that complete tranquillity reigned at the University of Kazan. But the papers that made this announcement were forbidden, under pain of suppression, to mention in what manner the pacification was brought about—that the rebellious students were beaten, whipped, thrown on the ground, dragged about by the hair of their heads, and, in many instances, hauled to prison. Despite the interdict laid on the Press, these facts were quickly bruited about. On November 8th (as is set forth in the official report) hectographic copies of a letter from one of the Kazan students, giving a full account of the affair, were circulated among the students of St. Petersburg, and caused naturally a great sensation. On the 10th hectographic circulars were issued calling a general meeting of the St. Petersburg students to protest against the outrages inflicted on their comrades of Kazan. When the students presented themselves at the place of meeting, the police, who were in great strength, ordered them to disperse, an order which they refused to obey, and while the police were still there passed a vote of censure on the authorities and of sympathy with the students of Kazan. On this force was ordered to be used, and 280 students were arrested and conducted to prison.

The next day orders went forth for the provisional closing of the university.

The outbreaks at St. Petersburg and Kazan were speedily followed by similar scenes in other university towns. On November 15th there were disturbances at Kieff, and on the 17th and 18th at Kharkoff. At the latter place the disturbances were so serious that the military had to be employed for their suppression, and many arrests were made. Almost at the same time troubles befel in the Juridical School of Yaroslavle, and a few days later at the Agricultural School of Moscow. At all these places events followed in the same order—agitations, meetings, forcible dispersions, arrests, and then provisional cessation of lectures.

Disorders are of frequent occurrence in all the universities and superior scholastic institutions of the empire. Hardly a year passes that several do not come to pass in different parts of Russia. And every one of these outbreaks, whether appeased by the exhortations of the professors or suppressed by Cossack whips, entails inevitably the expulsion of a crowd of students. In some cases fifty are expelled, in others one hundred, and even more than one hundred. The troubles of October and November, 1882, caused the expulsion of six hundred. The tribunal which orders the expulsions—that is to say, the Council of Professors—divides the offenders into several categories. The "leaders" and "instigators" are condemned to perpetual expulsion and denied the right of entering thereafter any superior school whatever. Others are expelled for a term varying from twelve months to three years. The lightest penalty awarded in these cases is "sending away," a sentence which, in theory at least, does not prevent the offender from entering at once some other university. In reality, however, there is very little difference between one sort of punishment and another. "The police," says the report of the St. Petersburg professors which I have already cited, "regard every disturbance that occurs in the university as a political movement." Every student who may be condemned, even to a slight punishment, becomes a political suspect, and to every Russian suspect there is dealt the same measure— exile by administrative order. Penalties inflicted for the merest breaches of scholastic discipline may be aggravated by administrative exile, as the disorders of March 18 and 20, 1869, clearly showed. All the students "sent away" for a year, as well as those definitively expelled, were immediately exiled; and after the late disturbances (December, 1878) the rector was asked to furnish the Chief of Police of the quarter with the names of all students who had ever appeared before the university tribunal, even though they might not have been punished (in order that they, too, might be exiled).

If in other parts of Russia the police are less severe than in St. Petersburg, students compromised by participation in university disorders are none the less dealt with in a way which renders impossible the resumption of their professional studies.

The Minister himself undertakes the task of tracking and marking them. Here is an instance in point. In a weekly journal, published at St. Petersburg, there appeared, on November 9, 1881, under the heading "An Incomprehensible Decision of the University Council of Kieff," a communication to the following effect—

"The students provisionally expelled (rusticated) from Moscow University applied for admission to the University of Kieff. But the Council, after taking the matter into consideration, refused to receive them. This was virtually increasing, on their own motion, the punishment originally inflicted on the postulants. It was denying a right reserved to them by their judges."

And the Press, generally, blamed the Council for displaying a severity which was qualified as excessive and inexplicable. The explanation, however, was very simple. The Minister, by a special circular, had forbidden all other universities to receive the expelled students from Moscow. This the papers knew better than anybody else, and these diatribes had no other aim than to provoke the University of Kieff into an exposure of the double dealing of the Government, an object which, it is hardly necessary to say, was not realized. Similar circulars are almost invariably sent out after university disturbances wherever they may happen to occur.

The struggle between the Ministry and the universities is far from being limited to disorders and their results. These events after all are exceptional, they occur at comparatively long intervals, and are separated from each other by periods of apparent calm. But quietness brings the students no immunity from espionage and persecution. The police never cease making arrests; when clouds darken the political sky, and the Government, with or without reason, take alarm, they arrest multitudes. At these times students are naturally the greatest sufferers, for, as I have already shown, our Russian youths are nearly all eager politicians and potential revolutionists. A fraction of the arrested are condemned, even after trial, to divers penalties. Some 80 per cent. are exiled, without trial, to Siberia or to one of the northern provinces; a few, after a short detention, are allowed to return to their homes. A proportion of those sentenced to a term of imprisonment may also be allowed to resume their occupations, instead of being exiled by administrative order. But mercy is a quality unknown to the Russian police; they take back with one hand what they give with the other. On October 15, 1881, a law was made instituting a sort of double judgment and twofold penalty for students coming under the categories last named. Articles 2 and 3 of this law direct university councils to act as special tribunals for the trial of students who have been tried and acquitted by the ordinary courts, or who have expiated their offences by terms of imprisonment. This law prescribes that, in the event of the police certifying that a young man whose case is under consideration has acted "out of pure thoughtlessness and without evil intent," the council may either admit or expel him at their discretion. But should the police impute to him "perverse intentions," albeit in a measure so infinitesimal that they do not deem it necessary to proceed against him themselves, the council must nevertheless pronounce a sentence of perpetual expulsion and deprivation of the right to enter any superior school whatever. Article 4 explains that the preceding articles apply not alone to students who have fallen under the lash of the ordinary law, but also to those who have escaped undamaged from the exceptional "law of public safety"—in other words, from the martial law, which has become one of Russia's permanent institutions.

To obtain for those who have fallen into the hands of the police any remission of their ostracism is a matter of excessive and almost insuperable difficulty. Requests for indulgence must be made to the Emperor personally—how many students have friends at Court?—and are only entertained when the suppliant can *prove* that during two years after his liberation or the definitive expiation of his offence *he has repented him of his errors*, and entirely broken with his old companions.

But apart from the juridic absurdity of a condition in contradiction with the accepted maxim that it is crime, not innocence, which must be demonstrated, how, we ask, can repentance be proved, if not by treachery or betrayal, or some service rendered to the police? And it may be safely affirmed that the law touching the expulsion of students acquitted by the courts, or who have undergone the punishments assigned to them, notwithstanding its seeming moderation, is absolute. The police never pardon; and even if that body and martial law allowed them to live freely in society the interdict on their university career would still remain.

Such are the true forms assumed by the veritable war which, sometimes open, sometimes latent, has for more than twenty years been waged between the youth of our superior schools and the Government of the country.

III.

But these are the merest palliatives. What has this ruthless persecution of a quarter of a century effected? Nothing at all. Despite arrests and banishments the students are as hostile to the Government as before. The fate of those who go down in the struggle serves not in the least as a warning to the survivors. More than ever are universities breeders of discontent and centres of agitation. And is there not something in the nature of things which necessarily produces this result? For what is higher education if not the study of European culture—its history and its laws, its institutions and its literature? And a man who has gone through a university course and studied these things can hardly be kept in the belief that Russia is the happiest of all possible countries, and her government the perfection of human wisdom. So, to destroy the evil at its roots, it is imperative to strike, not men alone, but institutions. This Count Tolstoi, as a far-seeing man, has long felt, though it is only of late that circumstances have permitted the practical application of his sagacious counsels. In the result the universities were attacked in two quarters—the high and the low. To begin with, Count Tolstoi made a strenuous effort to reduce the number of students by increasing academic fees and rendering examinations absurdly severe. When this measure did not abate the flood of young men eager for instruction, the Count (by a ministerial order under date of March 25, 1879) arbitrarily deprived seminary pupils (who formed a large proportion of the undergraduates) of the right of admission to the universities, a right they had enjoyed from time immemorial. At Odessa the proportion of these youths was from a third to a half of the total number of undergraduates. Thus the new law wielded by Count Tolstoi did yeoman service.

Yet still he was not satisfied, and other measures, whose vandalism was cynical and complete, were instituted, measures which mutilated to the verge of extinction the system of superior education.

The first to feel the effect of these measures was the Medico-chirurgical Academy of St. Petersburg. Than this there is no institution in the empire more useful to the State. It is under the Ministry of War, and supplies the army with surgeons, of whom during the conflict with Turkey there was so lamentable a lack. But the medical school, with its one thousand students, was a centre of political agitation, and an Imperial ukase, dated March 24, 1879, doomed it to complete transformation and semi-extinction. The number of students was diminished to five hundred, the terms reduced from five to three, and the two first courses, the undergraduates belonging to which were the most unruly, were abolished.

The only students now received are those who have passed two terms at a provincial university. They are paid, wear a uniform, take the oath of allegiance, and from the day of their admission are considered as forming part of the army, and held amenable to military law. At the instance of the Minister of War the five years' course has lately been re-established, but the other repressive measures are maintained in all their rigour.

On January 3, 1880, another ukase ordered a similar transformation of the Institute of Civil Engineers. This mutilation of a useful school lessened by one-half the few openings in life available for the pupils of our non-classical gymnasiums.

A little later came the turn of the Female Medical School of St. Petersburg. This school, founded in 1872, proved eminently useful. In Russia the supply of medical men is utterly inadequate for the needs of its vast population. Doctors, being much sought, naturally settle by preference in the towns where their services bring the best return. With rare exceptions, the rural districts are left a prey to bloodletters, bone-setters, quacks, and sorcerers. Women, on the other hand, settle by preference in the country, and are content with such moderate fees as the Zemstvo can afford. The Female School of Medicine was thus a great boon; requests for women doctors were continually being received from all parts of the country; and when, in April, 1882, the Government announced that, "for pecuniary reasons," they would be compelled to close the school, there was a general expression of surprise and regret. The papers protested as much as they dared; the Zemstvo remonstrated; the municipality of St. Petersburg and several scientific corporations offered annual subsidies; private individuals, both rich and poor, and even obscure villages, offered subscriptions towards the maintenance of so valued an institution. But the Female School of Medicine was doomed, and in August, 1882, appeared an ukase ordering its abolition. Students already admitted might complete their course, but no new pupils were allowed to be taken. The cause assigned for this proceeding was the shallowest of pretexts; the true reason being a fear on the part of the Government that the school might become a seminary of revolutionary ideas.

Not less characteristic was the conduct of Government in the matter of the Polytechnic Institution of Kharkoff. The only establishment of the sort in Russia is that of St. Petersburg, and thither all youths desirous of being educated in the mechanical arts must proceed. In a country so vast this is highly inconvenient, and for a long time past Kharkoff had wanted to have a Polytechnic of its own. At length, after repeated applications to the Minister of of Public Instruction and negotiations extending over ten years, the authorization was granted; whereupon the municipality erected a suitable building, appointed a staff of professors, and all was ready to begin, when the Government suddenly changed their mind, withdrew the authorization, and forbade the school to be opened—on the ground that they saw no necessity for any establishment of the sort. Nor was this all. They offered the building, which had cost Kharkoff 50,000 roubles, as a present to the university; but the university, making common cause with the town, declined the offer. The building is still in the hands of the State, and will, it is rumoured, be turned into a cavalry barrack.

At length, and only a few months ago, came the long-expected blow which struck our universities in another vital point—the Regulation of September, 1884, whereby was definitively abolished the Regulation of 1863.

There are few recent questions which have so greatly excited public opinion in Russia, and given rise to so much heated polemic in the Press as that of the abolition of the Regulation of 1863. It was a Regulation which, by permitting the professors to fill up vacant chairs and elect the members of the managing body, conferred on the universities a fair measure of autonomy and independence. Mr. Katkoff, who is one of the most influential men in the empire, and whose particular friends of the Moscow University have not found this independence to their advantage, entertained for the unfortunate Regulation of 1863 a mortal hatred. For years it was his *Delenda Carthago*.

He protested against it in season and out of season. To hear him you would think this Regulation was the cause of all the so-called " disorders " and most of the misfortunes of the last twenty years. Sedition (Nihilism) in his opinion derives its chief support from the autonomy of the universities. The process by which he arrives at this conclusion is short and simple. The majority of the professors being secret ministers of subversive ideas (rather a strange confession for a friend and defender of the Government), to leave them free to choose their colleagues is to maintain at the expense of the State a permanent revolutionary propaganda. But this argument, however ingenious, was rather too farfetched to be used by the administration. A more plausible if not a more truthful pretext was necessary, something that might enable the Government to say that in abolishing the obnoxious Regulation they were promoting the best interests of the nation. The inventive genius of Mr. Katkoff was equal to the occasion. He developed from his inner consciousness the thesis that the abolition of the Regulation of 1863 would give an extraordinary stimulus to the study of science, and raise learning in Russia to a level with that of Germany. The idea being eagerly caught up by the official Press, it was soon made to appear that, in the interest of knowledge as well as of order, a new Regulation had become absolutely necessary.

Let us now examine a little this palladium of reaction, and see by what means it is proposed to effect the twofold object in question.

First of all, as to the police; for whenever anything happens in Russia the police are sure to be to the fore, and nobody doubts that the object of the present measure is simply repression. This is avowed by its advocates. "The universities," exclaimed the *Novoie Vremia*, "will no longer be corruptors of our youth. The universities will henceforth be guaranteed against disloyal intrigues." But will the new regulation be really to the advantage of learning? timidly whispered the so-called Liberal papers. All alike recognized the true character and aim of the measure.

We pass by the proposals for the supervision of the undergraduates, as to which nothing, or next to nothing, more remained to be done. That which gives a special savour to the new Regulation is placing the professors themselves under stringent police surveillance and arbitrary rule. Two institutions are charged with this ignoble duty. First of all the governing body, composed of professors; next the police of the inspection. Under the old system the rector and the four deans were simply *primus inter pares*, elected by their colleagues for a term of three years, after which others might be chosen to succeed them. Now they are masters, nominated by the Minister, and holding their lucrative places at his pleasure. As, moreover, among fifty or sixty men there must necessarily be some sycophants and self-seekers, the Minister has no difficulty in finding rectors who will take his orders and do his bidding. Under the new dispensation the rector, now become a Government agent, is clothed with extensive powers. He can convoke and dissolve at his pleasure the university council, once the supreme governing body. It is he alone who decides whether the proceedings of the council are according to rule, and by simply pronouncing it irregular he may quash any resolution to which he objects. The rector may also, if he thinks fit, preside with the same prerogatives at the meetings of the faculties. Like a commander-in-chief, wherever he appears he is supreme. The rector is also enjoined to make any observations to the professors he may deem necessary, and reprimand them whenever he sees fit. Every part of the administrative machine is open to his inspection, either in person or by deputy. Finally, paragraph 17 gives him, in cases of urgency, the right "to take any measures he may think expedient for the maintenance of order in the university, even if they exceed his powers." This article has evidently in view the so-called "disorders," which it is the custom in Russia to put down by military force. But almost any construction might be placed upon the clause, and there is hardly any measure, however extreme, which it could not be held to sanction.

Thus Russian universities resemble rather fortresses whose garrisons are permeated by sedition, and ready at any moment to break into open mutiny than homes of learning and temples of science. The rector is the commander-in-chief. Under his orders are four deans, rectors of faculties, each exercising in his own department analogous functions, but chosen by the Minister, not by the rector. It is chiefly to the deans that the task is intrusted of overseeing the professors of their respective faculties; and to render the latter more dependent the new Regulation introduces important innovations in the method of their appointment. Before a man can become a professor he must henceforth serve three years as a tutor (*privat-docent*), and can only become a tutor on the nomination of the curator of the province, or on the proposal of the council of professors of the faculty of his choice. In any event the appointment must be confirmed by the curator of the province, and this functionary, who is a high official of the Ministry, may revoke any tutor's appointment without assigning a cause. A tutor's pay is only about a third of that of a full-fledged professor, and as he is subjected to an incessant surveillance to guard him against the contagion of subversive ideas the post cannot be considered a very desirable one; nor is it likely to attract young men of large views and independent mind.

To the rector and the deans falls the duty of seeing that the tutor's teaching is all that it ought to be. If his lectures are not in conformity with the dignity of his subject, or are found to be tainted with dangerous ideas, they must admonish him. Should the admonition prove ineffectual the rector will propose to the curator to dismiss this refractory tutor, and the curator will no doubt give prompt effect to the proposal. But if the curator should learn in some other way (through spies or a member of the inspection) that a tutor's lectures are showing subversive tendencies, he may be removed without reference to the rector. The new *privat-docents* have thus two or three sets of masters, and besides being at the mercy of the rector and his deputies, as also of the curator of the province, they are liable at any moment to be denounced by the inspector and his satellites. The least show of independence will insure their prompt dismissal, the more especially as being only young in the scholastic profession they are not likely to command the respect of their superiors. For promotion they depend entirely on the Minister and his agents.

Formerly the professors were nominated by the council of the faculty. True, the Minister had the power of veto, but he had no power of appointment, and if one man was rejected the council had only to nominate another. According to the new scheme, however, the Minister can appoint to a vacant chair "any scholar possessing the necessary qualifications" —that is to say, any one who has served the prescribed time as a *privat-docent*. The Minister may, if he likes, consult the heads of the university, but only if he likes. He may equally, if he likes, consult a private friend or a member of the inspection. The promotion of a professor from the second to the first class—a change which brings with it increased emoluments—also rests entirely with the Minister.

Nor does this exhaust the enumeration of the Minister's powers. He nominates professors to examinerships, which from a financial point of view, and having regard to the new system of paying examiners, is a highly important function. Under the old system every professor was *ipso facto* an examiner; under the present, examinations are conducted by special commissions nominated by the Minister. Under the old, students paid a fixed yearly sum, which gave them the right of attending all the university lectures. According to the new regulations they have to pay each professor separately. In these circumstances, undergraduates, having the right of choice, naturally flock to the lectures of the professors by whom they are likely to be examined. Hence the placing of a professor on the examining commission makes greatly for his pecuniary advantage—brings him hearers and adds to his emoluments. The right of nomination is thus a very effective means of increasing the power of the Government over the teaching body. In a country such as Switzerland, where political motives are not allowed to influence collegiate appointments this system produces no injurious results; but experience proves that in Prussia its consequences are bad, and in Austria nothing less than disastrous. It is easy to understand, therefore, the motives of our Government in importing the system into Russia, and the effect it is likely to produce there.

"But where, then," the reader may ask, "is the teaching strength — where the science and other branches of higher culture? In what consists the reform which is supposed to confer on the measure its pedagogic character? Are we expected to believe that it consists in the new discipline imposed on long-suffering rectors, deans, and inspectors, the appointment of *privat-docents* and payment by lesson?"

All these things being, in name at least, borrowed from Germany, they are expected in some mysterious fashion to render teaching more efficient. If we could have the freedom of German universities, their methods might perhaps be adopted with advantage, but the form without the spirit can profit nothing.

To all who are not blinded by self-interest, it is evident that the new Regulation must prove fatal to all true learning—freedom and independence being as essential to its prosperity as atmospheric air to physical life. By making political orthodoxy the only sure qualification for all higher university appointments, the intellectual *élite* of the nation is almost necessarily excluded from their walls. The old system of Government interference drove from their chairs some of our best professors—Kostomarov, Stasulevitch, Pipin, Arseniev, Setchenov, and many others—all moderate men, who had retained their positions with honour for years, and were guilty of only one fault—that of maintaining their personal dignity and the dignity of their calling, and refusing to prostrate themselves before the despotism of a Minister. That which was formerly an exceptional abuse of power has now become a rule. The professors have been converted into *tchinovniks*—an odious name, despised by all our Russian youth—and their characters and qualifications will soon be in strict conformity with their new rank; one by one all true scholars will abandon their chairs, and the Government, in the exercise of its rights, will fill them with its creatures. In default of men of high scientific acquirements, the old professors will be succeeded by tutors and *soi-disant* scholars—whom the curators are at liberty to choose from among persons that have not even undergone the examinations ordained by the faculty—" provided they are favourably known by their works," as to the merit of which his excellency the curator is the sole judge.

CHAPTER XXVII.

SECONDARY EDUCATION.

I.

THE war of Russian Governments against higher education, described in the foregoing chapter, is of long standing. It began in the time of Alexander I., during the reaction produced by the murder of Kotzebue by the student Sand, which, originating in Germany, spread quickly over the whole of Continental Europe. In the reign of Nicolas, a period of uninterrupted reaction, the universities were always under the special charge of the Third Section. In order, as he hoped, to counteract the pernicious effects of liberal culture, the Tzar organized the universities like battalions, and lectures in the class-room was followed by drills in the square. Knowledge he regarded as a social bane, and military discipline as its only antidote. The absurd Regulation in question was suppressed by his son, whose reign began so brightly and ended so terribly. Alexander II. loosened the fetters which his father had imposed, and for some time after he ascended the throne learning breathed freely and made marked progress. But in 1860, when "disorders" and "manifestations" occurred in the universities of the two capitals, the authorities took alarm, repressive measures were adopted, and since that time the struggle between the State and the flower of our Russian youth has gone on with ever-increasing virulence. The war against secondary education —for war it has become—is of more recent date. On April 4, 1866, Karakosoff fired the fatal revolver shot which confirmed, as it would seem for ever, the resolution of the Government to follow the dangerous path of reaction and repression.

"You are a Pole, are you not?" asked the Tzar, when Karakosoff was led before him.

"No; I am a Russian," was the answer.

"Then why did you try to kill me?" demanded the astonished sovereign. So difficult did he find it at that time to believe that any other than a Pole could make an attempt on his life.

But Karakosoff told the truth; he was one of the Tzar's own Russian subjects, and the subsequent inquiry, directed by Mouravieff, showed that many of

Karakosoff's former fellow-students sympathized with his objects and shared in his ideas.

The effect of this attempt, and the discovery to which it led, were decisive. The Polish insurrection, as is well known, converted Alexander II. to reactionary views. But it now became evident that the reactionary measures adopted in 1863 had proved abortive, and that the revolutionary fermentation was increasing. Yet, instead of inferring therefrom that the fault of this failure lay with the new policy of reaction, the very opposite conclusion was drawn—that the reins must be still further tightened. It was then that the reckless reactionary party brought forward the man of fate, Count Dmitry Tolstoi, whom posterity will call the scourge of Russia and the destroyer of the autocracy.

This paladin of absolutism was entrusted with plenary powers for the purification of the schools of the empire from social heresy and political discontent.

How he dealt with superior education we have already told. Yet he only strengthened and enforced the system which his predecessors had for a long time practised. To him alone, however, belongs the questionable honour of "purifying"—according to his lights—first of all secondary, and afterwards primary education. It was especially in relation to the

SECONDARY EDUCATION. 113

former of these branches that the inventive genius of the man shone the most brilliantly. His fundamental idea was perfectly just—that thoroughly to "purify" the universities he must go first to the fountain-head and purify the gymnasiums, from which they draw their yearly tribute of students. So Count Tolstoi set himself to purge these institutions, which, of course, meant handing them over to the tender mercies of the police; and it is a positive fact that Russian schoolboys of from ten to seventeen years of age may now be punished for so-called political offences and for holding erroneous political opinions. No longer since than September, 1883, the Minister of Public Instruction issued a circular in which it was stated that in thirteen gymnasiums, one pro-gymnasium, and ten "real" schools, there had been discovered traces of a criminal propaganda, and that in fourteen other gymnasiums and four "real" schools there had taken place "collective disorders"—whatever that may mean. All these establishments were ordered to be placed under special police oversight.

It is difficult for a stranger to realize the extent to which espionage is carried on in our gymnasiums. The pedagogues, who ought to enjoy the respect of their pupils, and imbue the rising generation with sentiments of honour, are transformed into agents of the Third Section. The boys are under continual supervision. They are not left in peace even in the houses of their kinsfolk. By a special law, tutors are ordered to visit the pupils at their own homes, or wherever they may be living. The Minister is not ashamed from time to time to issue circulars, as on July 27, 1884, cynically offering rewards and promotion to professors who show the greatest zeal in supervising the "moral dispositions" (read "political tendencies") of their pupils, and threatening that in the event of any anti-governmental propagandism being discovered in their classes, they will be held equally responsible with the directors and inspectors (*Rousskia Vedomosti,* July 28th)—which means money and advancement for those who play the part of spies, dismissal for those who refuse to bow the knee to Baal.

II.

But measures of police are not enough; they must be backed up by measures of prevention. Boys must be removed from every influence that might predispose them to pernicious ideas, such as socialism, liberty, materialism, and so forth. To this end the pedants of the Third Section drew up a series of prescriptions known as the Gymnasial Regulations of 1871, which are still in force. The explanatory appendix to the Regulations says roundly that "the less history is studied in the gymnasiums the better." The study of Russian literature is also banned by Count Tolstoi; and general geography, on account of its "dangerous tendencies," is proscribed by the Minister of Instruction. It may "suggest conflicting conclusions and give rise to useless reasonings." In other words, the study of geography may peradventure lead to discussions on political and social subjects. For these reasons the Regulations of 1871 diminished the number of lessons in history, geography, and Russian. The void made by these omissions has been filled up with the learned languages. The panacea is found in Greek and Latin. The gymnasiums have become classic, and nothing but classic. The first class of a Russian gymnasium (composed of boys of ten years old) has now eight Latin lessons a week; the third the same in Latin and as many in Greek. All other subjects are declared secondary, and though not ostensibly forbidden, persistently discouraged. However many bad marks pupils may receive in their mother tongue, in history, mathematics, geography, foreign languages, or even in religion, they never fail to obtain their promotion to a higher class, but backwardness in the classical languages is punished by expulsion.

Is it however the fact, that study of the classics serves as a safeguard against "perverse," in other words, liberal and humane, ideas? Certainly not. Great authorities hold, and John Stuart Mill has said, that serious study of the lives and history of the peoples of antiquity makes more for the development of moral and civic virtues than the study of modern history.

But we have no desire to discuss the advantages or disadvantages of classical education. Whichever way the balance may incline, it is quite certain that the classicism devised by Tolstoi, Katkoff, and consorts, is altogether *sui generis*, and can only stupify those whom it is supposed to enlighten. The effect of their regulations is to make grammar an end instead of a means. Scholars learn the language and nothing else. Their studies are simply a series of linguistic exercises.

Pedagogues *à la* Katkoff do not deny this. They merely contend that there is nothing so well suited for the development of the intelligence as the study of the dead languages. According to an expression of theirs which has been much in vogue, it is a mental gymnastic exercise which no other study can equal. With this inscrutable word "gymnastic" they meet all the arguments of their adversaries. Thus for seven years past the youth of Russia have been doing nothing but gymnastics, whose uselessness is admitted by teachers and bitterly deplored by parents.

The effect of the system on pupils is nothing less than disastrous. Boys of ten and eleven years old, who are compelled to give sixteen hours a week to a language so different from their own as Latin, end by conceiving for it such a distaste and disgust that its study becomes painful and unproductive. The examinations for removes are moreover made so difficult —by special order of the Minister—that an immense number of boys fail to pass them, and are summarily expelled. According to the report of the Department of Instruction for 1879, which gives the results for the seven years then ending, 6511 pupils only had completed their course during that period, while no fewer than 51,406 had either been expelled for failure to satisfy the examiners or abandoned the attempt in despair. The chances against a boy in the first (lowest) class going through all the upper classes, and so being able to enter a university, are nine to one; that is to say, eight-ninths are rejected. Of the second class three-fourths fail, of the third two-thirds, and of the select few who successfully run the gauntlet and reach the seventh class one-fourth break down in their final examination.

These figures tell their own tale. The system is not a test of fitness; it is a massacre of innocents.

The plan invented by Count Tolstoi dooms thousands of children to ignorance and deprives many of them of all chance of a useful career. And it cannot be urged on behalf of the Government that they are unaware of the evil which it works and the discontent which it causes. For years past the Press, fettered as it is, has never ceased to protest against the new system of education and the deplorable consequences which it entails. Despairing parents bewail the fate of their unfortunate children, and the growing frequency of suicides among boys of thirteen lends to their complaint a terrible significance. But the Government remains firm, and the massacre of innocents goes on.

But why, it may be asked, do parents continue to send their children to the shambles? Are there in Russia no other schools than these classical gymnasiums? There are. The new classicism is designed only for the well-to-do. The classical gymnasiums do not give a complete education. They are merely preparatory schools for the universities. To the numerous class who look to education for the means of ensuring their children a livelihood, the gymnasiums are of no use whatever. It is consequently necessary to throw them also a bone, and for their benefit have been founded the professional institutions known as "real" or "realist" schools. But there are very few of them—thirty-nine; while of gymnasiums and pro-gymnasiums there are a hundred and eighty.

At St. Petersburg, where practical instruction is so greatly needed, there are two "real" schools, as compared with sixteen classical gymnasiums and pro-gymnasiums, a state of things which proves that the Government has very little desire for the diffusion of instruction among the middle classes. But it is in the general organization of these schools that the ill-will of the Government is more particularly manifested. Their object, according to the original Regulation, is (1) to afford young men an education capable of immediate practical application; and (2) to prepare them for the higher professional schools; and these schools profess to devote much more time and attention to the study of the mother tongue, mathematics, and natural sciences, than the classical schools. Yet these studies, useful though they are as the foundation of a sound technical education, are purely theoretical; they do not alone conduce to any practical results. To remedy this defect, a supplementary class (the seventh) has been organized, which, however, remedies nothing. This class is composed of two sections—one mechanico-technical, the other chemico-technical. In these two sections, though the course is one year, all the practical scientific instruction is comprised within two months and ranges over many subjects—mechanics, chemistry, mines engineering—everything, in fact, so that it is hardly possible for a pupil to get even a smattering, much less an efficient knowledge of any one of them.

The confusion which this system must needs entail is self-evident. These are not courses—rather a *catalogue raisonné* of every sort of science, a harlequin performance, a kaleidoscope composed of fragments of everything. The result is, that when pupils have passed through this supplementary class, they are no more capable than before of applying practically any of the scientific knowledge they are supposed to have acquired. A manufacturer never thinks of employing in his establishment a "realist" graduate, for the latter's pretended science is inferior to that of an overlooker or workman who has been taught solely by personal observation and experience.

Russian commerce requires only men of inferior education, but without diplomas none can become schoolmasters and instructors. Yet comparatively few either obtain diplomas or complete their studies in the superior technical schools, the reason being that there is not a sufficiency of these institutions to receive the pupils sent up by the "realist" gymnasiums. According to the report of the Minister of Public Instruction, published in 1879, the thirty "real" schools having the seven classes turned out 330 students fully qualified for admission to the superior schools. But as the latter had room for no more than 151, less than half could be received, and the greater part were consequently rejected. And these "real" school scholars are far from being the only candidates for admission to the four superior professional schools. In the year 1879 alone, for instance, there were no fewer than 380 applicants for admission to one technical school which could accommodate only 125. In No. 2638 of the *Novori Vremia* a professor, in warning young men in the provinces not to count too confidently on being able to enter these institutions, mentions that out of one thousand candidates who in 1883 presented themselves for admission into the two schools of industry and mines, no more than two hundred could be received, the rest having to be rejected simply for lack of room. But despite warnings and discouragements, so great is the eagerness of our youth for superior instruction that they still apply in crowds for admission to the schools, only to meet, time after time, with the same rebuffs and the same disappointments. The demand for professional instruction in Russia arises not alone from a thirst for knowledge, but from a natural desire to develop the great natural riches of the country, to which end a measure of technical education is absolutely necessary.

But the Government, so far from affording increased facilities for instruction, actually forbids the foundation of new colleges, as we have seen in the case of Kharkoff, and will not allow existing institutions to add to their accommodation. The motive of this dog-in-the-manger policy is the fear that, recruited as they are from classes comparatively poor, technical schools are more likely to become infected with subversive ideas than the classical gymnasiums of Count Tolstoi. The fate of the rejected among the "real" school men is very sad. Unable to enter the universities, and debarred from the callings for which they were destined, the greater part of them "remain in the streets." Well may they call themselves the "Minister's bastards," for while youths from the classical schools, once they have matriculated, are received everywhere, the luckless "realists" are rejected everywhere; against them all doors are closed. Yet neither society nor the Press can either rest indifferent to the troubles of these unhappy waifs, nor ignore the national loss entailed by the running to waste of so much intellectual energy. Their position has been the theme of hundreds of articles, written in the cautious and measured language which an imperious necessity imposes on Russian journalists. The best and most natural solution of the difficulty would be the enlargement of existing technical colleges and the re-establishment of new ones; but this being evidently out of the question, no more is asked than that matriculated "realists" may be allowed to enter the universities and graduate in medicine, science, or mathematics, for which they are far better prepared than their *confrères* of the gymnasiums, whose acquisitions are limited to Latin and Greek. It will hardly be believed that even this modest request was refused. In 1881 the Zemstvo took action in the matter, and, following the example of the Zemstvo of Tchernigoff, made a general demand for the admission of "realists" to the scientific faculties of the universities. The Ministry, not deeming it politic to reject peremptorily this petition, appointed a commission to whom the question was to be referred, and a time (January 19, 1882) was actually named for the first meeting. But on the 18th the members of the commission received a notification from the Minister that the meeting was to be adjourned indefinitely, and it stands adjourned to this day.

It is thus evident that the Government accepts without reserve all the most reactionary ideas of Count Tolstoi, who, unfortunately for our country, exercises a predominant influence over its domestic policy, and the Minister of Public Instruction has as evidently decided to deny, as far as he can, facilities for higher education to all whom lack of means compels to take to professional pursuits. It is this class, he thinks, which is most disaffected to the State, and he would make superior instruction the exclusive appanage of the rich and noble, whose position, either as landowners or servants of the Tzar —if, urged by necessity, or prompted by ambition, they have entered the service of the State—constrains them to support the existing system.

III.

Unsatisfactory as the condition of our scholastic institutions—badgered by the Government, watched by the police, exposed to all sorts of demoralizing influences—may be, so great is the need of instruction, so eager are our youth for knowledge, that schools of every degree are besieged by applicants, willing to submit to all the conditions which the State may see fit to impose, but unable to obtain admission. That this is no overdrawn or partisan statement the following extract from the *Nedielia* of August 26, 1883, will show—

"The end of the summer vacation and the beginning of the scholastic year are marked by the usual chorus of complaints about the lack of vacancies in public schools, and parents are cruelly embarrassed in their efforts to procure suitable instruction for their children. As the facts set forth in country papers abundantly testify, this evil is by no means confined to one locality. None of the classical gymnasiums at Moscow have vacancies for first-class pupils. In those of St. Petersburg vacancies are extremely few. In the gymnasium of St. Petersburg no places whatever are to be had in the first-class; in the pro-gymnasium there are only six disposable places; in the first-class and in the real school there are no vacancies whatever, not even in the second-class."

At the Cronstadt Technical School there were 156 applicants and only 30 places. A correspondent writing from Kieff to the same paper mentioned that for every vacancy there were five postulants, for some classes there were eight and ten. The natural consequences of this state of things are excessive crowding and inefficient teaching. Masters are at their wits' end to find room for those whom they actually receive. At every desk there are four boys instead of two. According to the *Saratoff Gazette* there were sixty-six applicants for thirty-seven places in that town, and the masters, shrinking from the invidious task of personal selection, made the candidates contend by competitive examination for the vacancies at their disposal.

These citations, which might easily be multiplied, will give a fair idea of the relation of supply to demand in the domain of Russian secondary education. The same story comes from every part of the empire, and this has been going on for years. It is a virtual denial of education to thousands of Russian youth, for, as I have already mentioned, there is no room for private effort in the dominions of the Tzar. The Government, which throws away scores of millions in Court festivals and distant wars, spares only a poor ten millions for purposes of education. And yet, in spite of its mania for repression and the resolute will of Count Tolstoi, the Government is forced from time to time to make concessions, often, however, more in name than reality. Every class is interested in the education of its youth. For the higher orders, without distinction of political opinion or social position, for Government *employés* as well as for ordinary citizens, the question is one of life and death. For if their children be not instructed, how can they live? And these classes combined, albeit possessed of no recognized political influence, are able, up to a certain point, to force the hands of Government. But when the Government yields to pressure, it yields reluctantly and slowly, and with the worst possible grace. For instance, during the last ten years, notwithstanding increase of population and the ever-growing demand for greater educational facilities, the credit for the gymnasiums has been increased by only 1,400,000 roubles on an expenditure of six millions, a sum altogether and ridiculously inadequate for the needs which it is supposed to satisfy. Tired of pestering the Government with petitions and complaints, some of the municipalities and the Zemstvo lately took the extreme resolution of building new classical gymnasiums, burdening their modest budgets with an outlay which ought really to be borne by the State. The expenditure of the Zemstvo of eighteen provinces on secondary education amounts to from 25 to 30 per cent. of the total sum assigned by these bodies for public instruction in general. This proves to what point the Government has carried its policy of opposition to the extension of middle-class instruction.

The policy of the Minister of Public Instruction as touching secondary schools may be thus summarized:—(1) To oppose by every possible means the diffusion of secondary education, to render it as difficult as possible, and make no concession save at the last extremity, when all the means of resistance have been exhausted. (2) When resistance becomes impossible, to try to exclude from the benefits of secondary education the professional classes (to whom it is a matter of life and death), in order to confine it, as far as may be, to the higher nobility and richer citizens. (3) The privilege once granted to these classes, to make the instruction given to their children as sterile as possible, and so arrange matters that it may be imparted to the fewest number.

These conclusions read more like a bad joke than

stern reality, yet are they not fully justified by the facts we have cited—facts, be it remembered, taken from official documents or from a censured and semi-official Press?

CHAPTER XXVIII.

PRIMARY INSTRUCTION.

I.

Primary instruction in Russia is of very recent growth, dating no further back than from the emancipation of 1861. It is true that great proprietors and serf-owners used to let a few of their thralls learn enough to become stewards and book-keepers. But, on the well-understood principle that educated slaves make dangerous servants, the mass of the rural population were deliberately left in the deepest ignorance. On the domains of the Crown alone were there a certain number of primary schools, but being placed under the supervision of the priests and the *tchinovnik*; who had neither the time nor the wish to look after them, they fell into a state of utter inefficiency. The few pupils they had learnt little or nothing, and more often than not the schools themselves were purely imaginary, "they existed only on paper," as we say in Russia—in other words, they were to be found only in the reports of the administration, in whose accounts always figured divers sums, supposed to have been paid for teachers' salaries and repairs of buildings, sums which, it is hardly necessary to say, went into the bottomless pockets of the *tchinovniks* and their accomplices. When the schools were afterwards made over to the Zemstvo, the frauds of this sort that came to light were absolutely appalling. At St. Petersburg (in 1872), when the management of the popular schools was handed over to the municipality of the capital, three, out of a nominal sixteen, were missing, They had never existed; the very names of them were fictitious. Of the remainder one alone was tolerably efficient, the remainder being badly organized and destitute of nearly every facility for study. The first proceeding of the municipality was to provide fresh buildings, furnish the schools with books, appoint a new and competent staff of teachers, and organize everything afresh. Yet these schools were founded more than a hundred years ago by the Empress Catharine, and had been ever since under the supervision of the State.

If this was the condition of primary instruction in

the capital, it is easy to understand what it must have been in the country. So far as it existed at all, it was due to private effort, either on the part of individuals or of the Zemstvo. The Government, as I shall presently show, did little then, and it does little now, but openly or covertly thwart the noble endeavours of Russian society to impart some slight degree of instruction to the masses of the people. In 1859 the instructed classes, roused to enthusiasm by the approach of emancipation, were eager for all sorts of reform, and, above all, to do something for their poorer fellow-citizens, so soon to be free. The idea of education took as much hold of the imagination of the youth of that day as did later the idea of a Socialist propaganda. But the establishment of children's schools was not enough to satisfy these aspirations. The effects of their teaching would not be manifest for a whole generation. What could be done to fit fathers and mothers for the boon of freedom and make them more worthy members of the new society? The question was answered and the want supplied by the creation of Sunday schools in every city, and in almost every town of the empire. The youth of both sexes threw themselves into the work with great ardour, and very soon excellent results were obtained. At Odessa alone six hundred persons offered themselves as teachers—of course without pay. But the Government viewed all this enthusiasm with dire alarm; there was no telling to what terrible consequences the mixing of the poor and the rich, the ignorant and the instructed might not give rise, and in the autumn of 1862 the Sunday schools were suppressed by order of the Tzar. And so ended a good work nobly begun. It was the first check imposed on the initiative of the public in this work. Popular instruction was again turned over to the priests and the *tchinovniks*, to the end that they might reduce it to a sham and a pretence.

In 1864, however, a step in the right direction was taken. The oversight of primary education was confided to the Zemstvo and other local bodies. In every district a School Board was constituted, of which three members were nominated by the Zemstvo and the municipality, and three elected by the Government. The Board was supervised by a provincial council composed of five members, of which two represented the Zemstvo and two the *tchinovniks*. The fifth member was the bishop, or his substitute, whose special duty it was to see that the character of the teaching in the popular schools was loyal and religious. The bishop received his information and gave his advice through the village priests, who were authorized to visit the schools and direct the masters, and if the latter did not conform to their counsel to make formal complaint against them. But as neither the bishop nor the *tchinovniks* gave much thought to the matter, rarely attending the meetings of the council, the management of the schools was left virtually to the Zemstvo. The new Regulation was thus much more liberal and popular than its authors meant it to be, and offered great facilities for the establishment of primary schools. The greatest difficulty encountered by the Zemstvo was paucity of funds, their expenditure being limited to a twentieth of the ordinary revenues. Yet stirred by a noble zeal for education the Zemstvo did wonders. In 1864 the number of primary schools was 17,678 with 598,121 pupils. We have now 25,000 schools with 1,000,000 scholars. But the progress achieved was even greater than these figures denote. The quality of the teaching was vastly improved. The old teachers were composed chiefly of sacristans, church singers, and old soldiers, most of whom could hardly read, much less write or cipher. To remedy this evil the Zemstvo started teachers' training schools, and raised the pay of the teachers from fifty to sixty roubles a year to an average of two hundred roubles, in exceptional cases to three hundred and three hundred and fifty roubles. Courses in pedagogy were also organized by which teachers could profit during the holidays, and by these means the efficiency of the schools was improved beyond measure. Though no general statistics are obtainable as to the results of the new departure, some suggestive facts and figures are to be found in the reports of the Zemstvo of Novgorod, Moscow, Samara, and a few other districts.

Of the present teaching staff about one-third have received a superior education in the middle class schools and seminaries, another third holds certificates from the normal college, and the remainder are men of the old school. From their modest revenues of 18,000,000 roubles the Zemstvo spare 4,000,000 for purposes of education; while from its revenue of 360,000,000 the Imperial Government spares for the same object only a million and a half, and of this sum 300,000 is taken by the inspection— that is to say, by the police of the schools. The country population—freed serfs and their children —whom many consider hopelessly ignorant and brutalized, and unfitted for any public function, show an almost pathetic eagerness to secure for their little ones the benefits of education. Notwithstanding their proverbial poverty, our rural communes voluntarily contributed as much towards the maintenance of the primary schools as the Zemstvo and the Government put together. Of the total amount (about $7\frac{1}{4}$ million roubles) required for these schools, the peasants pay 41, the Zemstvo 34, the

Imperial Government 14, and private individuals, mostly landowners, 11 per cent. And it is a fact of much significance that the provinces which make the greatest sacrifices for the promotion of education are exactly those in whose Zemstvo the peasants have the greatest proportion of deputies. The towns, too, and, above all, St. Petersburg, have made strenuous efforts to popularize education. The thirteen wretched schools of 1864, with a few score pupils, had grown in 1882 to 158 excellent establishments with a staff of certificated teachers and 6000 scholars of both sexes. The province of Tamboff, which, before the creation of the Zemstvo, had 174 primary schools with 7700 pupils, possess now 500 schools with an average attendance of 27,000 children. In 1860 Nijni Novgorod had 28 schools and 1500 scholars; twenty years later the Zemstvo of the province had organized 337 schools, in which nearly 12,000 children were receiving the rudiments of education. The progress thus achieved would be remarkable in any circumstances; if account be taken of the hostility of the Government and the difficulties thrown in the way of the Zemstvo by the official class, it seems prodigious. The Government shows scant favour to the universities and superior schools; to the primary schools it shows even less; and its treatment of them has been so unworthy of

the rulers of a great country that, if the facts I am
about to set forth were not proven—that is to say, if
they had not appeared in official reports and been
stated in newspapers over which is always hanging
the Damocles sword of censure and suspension—
they would seem nothing less than incredible, and I
should be accused of wilful exaggeration in repeating
them.

II.

The Zemstvo hardly began the work of reorganization when they encountered the opposition of the Ministry. Their most pressing need was good teachers. They wanted to be allowed—they asked nothing more—to establish teachers' colleges. After two years of waiting and dozens of petitions, Mr. Golovnine, the then Minister of Education, seemed to be on the point of giving the required authorization, when (in 1866) the first attempt to assassinate the Emperor came to pass—an event which was followed by the accession of Count Tolstoi to the Ministry and his assumption of the portfolio of Public Instruction. His first proceeding was to impose a peremptory veto on the proposed organization of teachers' colleges, and in his report to the Tzar, published in 1867, he takes special credit to himself for having burked so pernicious and revolutionary a scheme. In his opinion, normal schools, besides becoming centres of democratic agitation, would be the means of contaminating the minds of Russian children with subversive ideas. For five long years the Minister remained deaf to the prayers and remonstrances of the Zemstvo, who were compelled to get teachers where they could and to retain the services of many of the sacristans and old soldiers, who were hardly less ignorant than their own scholars. But the events of 1870 wrought a startling change, for it was said— and all believed—that the victories of Wörth, of Gravelotte, and of Sedan were won, not in the cabinet of General von Moltke, but in the schools of the Fatherland. Then it dawned on the minds of some of the Emperor's advisers, notably on that of the Minister of War, that men make none the worse soldiers for knowing how to read and write, and the interdict on the establishment of normal schools was removed. There are now sixty of them; but Count Tolstoi, while yielding to necessity, yielded reluctantly, and some of the Zemstvo—though their petitions have been incessant—have not even yet received the needful concession. But from their very inception these excellent institutions have been the objects of official jealousy and incessant suspicion, and are continually exposed to the double fire of the police of the State and the police of the Ministry of Education.

And a regard for truth constrains us to say that in this strife the Minister of Instruction displayed far greater zeal than the Third Section. The fate of our best schools of this class, founded by the efforts of the Zemstvo and the enterprise of private citizens (by Mr. Moksimov at Tver, Mr. Drouginine at Torjok, the Zemstvo of Riasan, and many others), destroyed for "admitting too many pupils," for "extending too largely the scholastic curriculum," for "reducing too much the charges for admission," and for other crimes of the same sort, are perfect illustrations of the spirit in which, for the last fifteen years, our so-called Minister of Instruction has conducted the business of his department and promoted the cause of education.

III.

The crusade against the universities is of long duration; that against the gymnasium and secondary education began in 1866. As for the primary schools, they remained for several years comparatively free from interference; but about 1874 it occurred to the Government that by preventing the seeds of disaffection from being sown in infant minds they might destroy Nihilism at its source. This idea was due to the discovery that several of the teachers were revolutionary emissaries. As a rule, these emissaries, in order the better to win over the working classes, assumed the character of common workmen, and actually worked as blacksmiths, masons, bricklayers, and labourers. A few, probably not more than a score, became teachers in village schools, their object being to carry on a propaganda among the peasants, certainly not to impart Nihilistic tenets to children struggling with the alphabet or deep in the mysteries of multiplication. This portentous discovery led to the placing of all the 25,000 schools of the empire under the ban of the police, and suggested to the Government the idea of the famous Regulations of 1874. The character and consequences of these Regulations were described by a St. Petersburg journal on November 2, 1880, shortly after the temporary disgrace of Count Tolstoi, when, during a brief space, it was possible for a paper to speak the truth without fear of prosecution or extinction, in the following terms—

"Alarmed by the spread of socialism in the provinces, Count Tolstoi, casting about in his mind for the cause of so portentous a phenomenon, came to the conclusion that the primary schools were the source of the mischief, and that the schoolmasters were the most formidable of revolutionary propagandists. So the Minister of Public Instruction, instead of favouring the creation of schools for the diffusion of exact knowledge and correct principles among the masses, began to put every obstacle in the way of this great work. He tried to protect the popular schools, as yet hardly established, from dangerous influences by measures much more likely to kill than to cure. In the eyes of Count Tolstoi our village schoolmasters, for the most part poor, ignorant, and inexperienced (it was only in 1871 that leave was given for the opening of teachers' training colleges), are enemies of the State and a danger to society, upon whom it is necessary to keep a perpetual watch with thirty-six eyes. Instead of being instructed in their duties, they are treated with contumely, and supervised like released malefactors. Instead of receiving the moral support of the authorities, they are cowed by threats; they know that the least display of spirit or of independence would bring them under suspicion of being politically heterodox; and their lives are made miserable by the knowledge that all their movements are watched, and that at any moment they may fall under the lash of the law for offences they wot not of."

"To keep in check enemies so redoubtable as these poor schoolmasters, it was clear that some agencies were needed even more powerful than the general police and the Third Section. So, under the form of provincial and district scholastic councils, Count Tolstoi created a police of his own, which it were no misnomer to call the political police of the primary schools. Nothing like it exists or ever did exist in any other country. Never were schools so watched, guarded, tutored, and controlled. Every children's school in the country is supervised, in the first line, by the governor of the province and the bishop of the diocese; then come the two ordinary councils, with their fifteen members, making a total of eighteen persons, all of them possessing large powers, though two only, the director and the inspector, have any special knowledge of pedagogy. [In this the writer is wrong. According to Article 20 of the regulations of 1874 these two only are authorized to direct the details of instruction, but it by no means follows that they have special qualifications for this duty; they are often, indeed, less competent than their *confrères*.] The surveillance of the other fifteen persons must therefore needs be almost purely inquisitorial."

Nor is this all. The author of the "Regulations," being apparently of opinion that fifteen inquisitors were not enough to safeguard the schools from political contamination authorized (Art. 41) the President of the Council to choose, at his discretion, from the nobility of the district, several private persons for the purpose of keeping an eye on the character of the instruction imparted in the primary schools, with special reference to its political tendencies. These persons, albeit no executive functions are conferred upon them, were invited to communicate their "observations and conjectures" (*sic*) to the President of the School Council—in other words, to play the spy. M. Kosheleff, one of the most respected members of our Zemstvo, said in an article printed in the *Zemstvo* (No. 2) that he doubted if there could be found in the whole of Russia a member of the nobility sufficiently servile to accept so ignoble a mission. But this renders the regulations in question neither less characteristic of the methods of our Government, nor the position of village schoolmasters more tolerable. The part refused by the gentlemen of the nobility is accepted by the *stanovoi* (constable) of the district, the *staroste* of the commune, or village innkeeper, any of whom may communicate his "observations and conjectures" to the school inspector, a proceeding that generally entails the poor schoolmaster's prompt dismissal.

"The position of our teachers," observes the priest

Kultchinsky in the *Samara Zemstvo*, "is really insupportable. They are controlled not alone by their many superiors, but by all the busybodies of a neighbourhood, in such a manner that it is quite impossible for them to satisfy demands so various and tastes so conflicting."

The following passage appears in the Report of the Commission of Inquiry of the Zemstvo of Chernigoff (1880)—

"The political element which of late has disturbed our provincial life has caused a number of persons and institutions to meddle with school affairs, from whose interference has followed no good results. Teachers find themselves at the mercy, not alone of a crowd of superiors, from the Marshal of the Nobility to the village priest, but of policemen, rural guards, and communal *employés*. Worried by so many masters, the teacher becomes incapable of performing his duties; he loses his head, and in order to obtain a little repose is often compelled to abandon his post."

It is also unfortunately the fact that the best men are the worst treated. The more a master is intelligent, instructed, and devoted to his duty, the more is he likely to be suspected by his superiors and denounced by some agent of the police as a fomenter of sedition and a corrupter of youth. If, on the contrary, he be ignorant and incapable, a drunkard and an idler, it is never imputed to him that he is a wolf in sheep's clothing, a revolutionist in disguise. The effect of the existing regulations is thus to drive from the schools the most competent teachers—a fact which is well understood by all the Zemstvo. It has even been publicly acknowledged by the School Council of Novgorod, who in an official report express surprise that any properly qualified teachers can be found ready to accept the conditions imposed upon them, and that it has been possible to achieve the very modest results already set forth.

IV.

And all this vandalism, this reign of terror, because among 25,000 teachers there have been found twenty or thirty apostles of sedition! Can it really be that the Russian Government is so ludicrously nervous as to tremble at the thought of a score or two, or even of a hundred, Nihilist emissaries being scattered over the length and breadth of the empire? Or is it only a pretext to hamper primary education? Pending an answer to this question I freely give the Government credit for all the stupidity which their conduct, on the hypothesis that they are sincere, inevitably implies.

But, as we shall presently see, its policy in the matter of popular instruction possesses a remarkable peculiarity which cannot be ascribed to fear of Socialism.

As I have already mentioned, the Regulations of 1864 placed the direction of the primary schools virtually in the hands of the local authorities. It was the best and most natural arrangement; it worked to the satisfaction of all; and the Zemstvo by their zeal, and the peasants by their contributions, showed themselves fully worthy of the trust reposed in them. But from 1869 the Government began, little by little, to undo the good they had done; by the Regulations of 1874 the local authorities were completely ousted from the management of the schools, and the *tchinovniks* ruled in their stead. The Zemstvo may pay if they like, for the payment is optional, but they have no longer any right to control the expenditure or take part in the direction, which is vested altogether in the nominees of the Minister; under the official designation of Inspector of Popular Schools. The power of these functionaries is little less than despotic. Without their authorization it is not permitted either to build a school-house, engage a teacher, begin a new course of instruction, or even purchase a primer. An inspector, by a mere stroke of the pen, can dismiss a master, close a school, or suppress a course of lessons. The so-called council may ask but they cannot require information touching the progress of the schools which they subsidize; the inspectors even refuse to communicate to them the results of the periodical examinations, for this, as one of these functionaries lately explained to the Zemstvo of the province of Taurida, would be admitting their right to meddle in matters which concern the inspectors alone. Thus the sole sphere of activity left open to the two councils is that of police; and it is a curious fact that albeit certain councillors may, if they discover anything politically suspicious, either dismiss a master, or shut up a school, they have no right either to recommend a manual or offer an opinion on the quality of the teaching or the progress of the scholars. And the inspectors, be it remembered, have no special qualifications for the positions which they occupy. "During the last few years," runs the report of the Zemstvo of Tchernigoff for 1881, "the inspection of our schools has become more stringent and less pedagogic. Among the new inspectors of primary schools is hardly to be found one who has received a superior education or obtained a certificate of proficiency as teacher. Some of them are men of phenomenal ignorance. Of one, a certain Mr. Jankovsky, the report of the Zemstvo of Berdiansk mentions that, during a public examination held in presence of the governor of the province, he showed utter ignorance of some of the simplest rules of arithmetic, such as are taught to children of tender age.

What, it may be asked, can be the cause of this reactionary policy of the Russian Government in regard to primary education? To push police supervision over the person of the schoolmaster to so absurd a length as that which I have described seems nothing less than a senseless freak of power. It is like burning down a house to rid it of mice. There is, nevertheless, a sufficiently obvious, yet utterly inadequate, reason for all these proceedings. The schoolmasters are generally young men, the mistresses young women, and the young being more receptive of new and strange ideas than the old, are therefore more likely to be contaminated with the pest of Nihilism. It is surely against them that the Government aim these measures of repression, even at the risk of destroying primary education altogether or rendering it inefficient to worthlessness. Yet this theory, though it may be good as far as it goes, does not explain why the management of the schools was taken out of the hands of the Zemstvo. For a proceeding so contrary to common sense no deep political motives can be assigned. It has never occurred even to the most suspicious of Ministers that the Zemstvo are capable of converting the schools into centres of a Socialist agitation. The Zemstvo are composed of landowners, priests, merchants, and *starchina* (rural mayors), none of them in the heyday of youth, or men whom even the most keen-scented of police functionaries can suspect of Socialist tendencies. It is true that they are not in favour of the present system. Every member of a Zemstvo, if he be not a traitor to his cause, must needs desire self-government and the free initiative of society—therefore political freedom more or less extensive. On the other hand, there has never been an instance of the Zemstvo using the schools for the propagation of—let us say—constitutional ideas. During the twenty-one years' existence of the thirty-four Zemstvo, no such charge as this has been brought against them.

We are thus driven to the conclusion that the reactionary measures of the Government are dictated by an instinctive dislike of education for its own sake, and a desire to check what they deem a too rapid enlightenment of the masses of the people. At first sight this conclusion may seem as extravagant as some other conclusions concerning the motives of the Russian Government, which, nevertheless, there is no evading. For in this regard the Government has the merit of being frank to cynicism, as the facts I am about to adduce abundantly prove.

The Regulation of 1874 strictly limits the instruction to be given in the primary schools. In other countries there is a *minimum* of education which all children must reach, in Russia there is a *maximum* beyond which they must not go. It is strictly forbidden to our little peasant children to acquire more than (*a*) an elementary knowledge of the catechism and of sacred history, (*b*) of reading and writing, and (*c*) of the four first rules of arithmetic. Over and over again have the Zemstvo besought the Ministry to let them enlarge a little this meagre curriculum, and give the poor little ones—some of them very intelligent and eager to learn—an idea of geometry, of decimals, and of the geography of the land they live in. All in vain ; these requests are either treated with contemptuous silence or answered with a peremptory negative. The same obscurantism explains the refusal of the Government to permit the use of any other language than Russian in the folk-schools of Finland, the Ukraine, and Poland, albeit the peasants of those countries know no tongue but their own. The consequence is that the children for the most part learn neither Russian nor anything else, which is probably what the authorities want.

The management of the schools under the present system, as must always be the case when a bureaucracy meddles with local affairs requiring special knowledge, is radically bad. The money spent on the 112 inspectors, which would suffice to maintain 700 new schools, is simply wasted. Each of the 112 has the care of 122 schools, and, as the primary schools make only about 156 working days in the year, it follows that the inspector of a district can give little more than one day during that time to each school—or could if they were close together. But seeing that they are generally spread over an area half as large as Ireland, destitute of railways and ill provided with roads, it is evident that no inspector, let him be ever so zealous, can give much more than an hour a year to each of the schools within his jurisdiction—even if he were to spend every moment of his waking hours in galloping over the length and breadth of his district.

These hardwrought civil servants, moreover, have a terrible amount of office work to get through. They are always writing and answering letters, making reports, and filling up returns. The inspector of Beloosero, when the Zemstvo complained that he never visited their schools, asked indignantly how they could expect him to do anything of the sort, seeing that he had to send off 2000 departmental and other business papers in the course of the year. In 1879 the Zemstvo of Novgorod complained that the inspectors had not time to visit even the model schools of the district, or be present at the examinations, to the great inconvenience of all concerned, none save the inspectors having power either to give orders or present reports. Similar complaints are continually made by other Zemstvo (for instance by those of Saraloff, Tchernigoff, Ekaterinoslav, and many more), and, though the latter have repeatedly offered to appoint supplementary inspectors at their own expense, they have not yet succeeded in prevailing upon the Ministry to accept this reasonable solution of the difficulty.

V.

The schools are thus in effect left without any true scholastic (as distinguished from political) oversight or direction whatever. The inspectors neither act themselves, nor let others act, and the Zemstvo are placed between the alternatives—watching with folded hands the destruction of their favourite work, and engaging in perpetual conflict with the agents of the State. Hence arise retrogression on the one hand, and endless contests with the inspectors on the other. The miserable history of our primary schools is that of an interminable war between these irreconcileable elements, a war in which the inspectors, backed by the Minister, always prevail. In a country so habituated to despotism, moreover, it is inevitable that the contest should often assume a character of pure vandalism. Of this the affair of Berdiansk, among others, offers a remarkable instance. Berdiansk was remarkable for its zeal in the cause of education; the best-schooled district in the well-schooled province of Taurida, only one of its eighty-eight primary schools was subsidized by the Government; all the rest were supported by the locality. It had no special inspector. The functionary who was charged with the duty, having two other districts to look after, could naturally give very little attention to any of them. So the Zemstvo, having no hope of being allowed to appoint a qualified school inspector of their own, resolved, if possible, to secure the services of a *tchinovnik* inspector. A request to this effect was forwarded to the Minister in due form, the Zemstvo offering, if it were granted, to pay the man's salary out of their own resources. For five years this modest request, though continually reiterated, remained unheeded and unanswered. But perseverance does wonders, and in the fifth year they were gratified by the appointment of a certain Mr. Garousoff, a favour for which they tendered the Minister their warmest thanks. But the Zemstvo were not long in finding out that they had made as great a mistake as the frogs who asked for a king and got a stork. The new inspector conducted himself like the master of a conquered country. "He annulled all the instructions and rules for the management of schools without substituting others, a proceeding which produced at first indescribable confusion ; and when (after some time), Mr. Garousoff's rules and prescriptions appeared, they were so contradictory that the teachers did not know what to do or whom to obey. He next, without any plausible pretext, dismissed and transferred from one place to another the best teachers. Alarmed by threats 'to throw them on the streets with a stroke of his pen,' which Mr. Garousoff continually repeated, the teachers began to leave the district. And when, to increase his power, the inspector brought against several of them political accusations—completely false, as was subsequently shown—the teachers were thrown into a veritable panic."

The Zemstvo complained to the director, as also to the Minister, and prayed to be relieved of the Vandal with whom the latter had presented them. But all in vain, and in the end the Zemstvo only got rid of their unloved inspector by a happy accident. He made a charge against a teacher of so outrageous a character that Todleben was constrained to dismiss him, and in October, 1879, Garousoff was succeeded by Jankovsky. But the Minister evidently held the district in detestation. Its schools were altogether too popular and successful. Jankovsky was no improvement on his predecessor. He dismissed teachers without cause, and when the Zemstvo protested against the discharge of a governess whom he had accused of Socialism, he threatened to accuse the entire Zemstvo of sympathizing with subversive ideas. He gave no heed to the wishes of the Zemstvo as to the management of the schools, saying that their only duty was the payment of his salary. He introduced so many changes into the scholastic course that the books did not arrive until the end of the year, when the course was over, and the schools were kept without teachers merely because the inspector did not take the trouble to confirm his appointment. This barbarous system lasted two years and did not terminate until the papers were filled with letters on the subject, and the schools of Berdiansk became the question of the day and a public scandal.

Were incidents like these of rare occurrence, they might, by a great stretch of charity, be ascribed to accident or official stupidity; but they are too frequent to be unintentional, and must be held to express, in deed, if not in word, the deliberate policy of the Ministry of Education. In the provinces of Tamboff, Ekaterinoslav, and many others, analogous facts have come to pass, and instances of conflicts between the Zemstvo and the inspectors, arising from similar causes, might be produced *ad infinitum*. In the session of 1879 the Zemstvo of Raizan presented an address of thanks to the five inspectors of the province for "having abstained from using the means at their disposal to thwart the Zemstvo in their efforts to promote primary education and increase the usefulness of the village schools." What irony could be more bitter, or what better proof be adduced of the determination of the Government to hinder, in every possible way, short of absolute suppression, the development of our popular schools? True, they have increased in numbers; but owing, on the one hand, to the absence of any real inspection, and, on the other, to frequent changes of system and dismissals of teachers, their efficiency is impaired to an extent that renders them powerless for good. In some instances the Zemstvo, weary of petitioning and remonstrating, have withdrawn their subsidies and left the schools to take care of themselves. During Count Tolstoi's temporary disgrace there was a hope of better things, and his successor, M. Sabouroff, was literally bombarded with petitions from all parts of the country, beseeching him to restore to the Zemstvo their liberty of action in the matter of education. But when, fourteen months later, Count Tolstoi returned to power as Premier and Minister of the Interior, all hope of amendment was at an end.

VI.

The Ministry of War has always shown more favour to education than the Ministry of Public Instruction, and, according to the law of conscription now in force, young men who have completed their course in a popular school are let off with four years' military service instead of six. But owing to the indifference of the peasants, arising from the obvious inefficiency of the schools, this clause has become almost a dead letter. "The condition of our schools," says the *Russian Almanack* for 1880, "is shown by the great number of pupils who abandon their studies before completing their course. In 1877 certificates were granted to no more than 88,255, equal to about eight per cent. of the total number of scholars." Figures like these are more eloquent than words. Only one scholar in twelve or thirteen succeeds in reaching the very low mark set by the examiners.

With this result the Government might surely have been satisfied, for they have virtually suppressed eleven schools out of twelve. But so far is this from being the case, that the Minister of Public Instruction contemplates a measure even more sweeping than the deposition of the Zemstvo—a measure which would be equivalent in the end to the entire suppression of primary instruction throughout the empire.* He proposes to take the schools out of the hands of the Zemstvo altogether, and to make the clergy the sole managers of primary education. He might as well propose to make the management over to the children; for the work would never be done, and the schools would perish of neglect. The clergy have neither time nor inclination for any other than their strictly clerical duties.

The Zemstvo of Kazan complained a little while ago that for two years the schools had not once been visited by a priest; formal complaints on the same score have been made by the Zemstvo of Moscow, Voronej, Tchernigoff, Tamboff, and St. Petersburg. In some provinces even the priests have met and passed resolutions to the effect that religious instruction can only be efficiently given by secular teachers, for even this duty it is quite out of the power of the clergy to perform. Nor when it is remembered that some of the parishes are so extensive that to give one lesson a week in each school would take two or three days, is this result very surprising. It is not given even to a priest to be in two places at one time. What would be the consequence of handing over the

---

* This was written before June 12, 1884.

schools to a class of men already so heavily burdened (to say nothing of their utter lack of pedagogic qualifications) may easily be imagined.

All this is well known to Count Tolstoi, both as ex-Minister of Education and ex-President of the Holy Synod. For my own part, I do not think that a scheme so monstrous can be carried into effect. There are limits even to the blindness and wickedness of an autocracy based on ignorance and buttressed by lies. But it is characteristic of the spirit which animates the advisers of the Tzar that a scheme so inimical to the best interests of the country should be seriously entertained.

* * *

I wrote thus in the *Times* in the spring of 1884, and I reproduce the foregoing lines by way of atonement for my want of foresight and the misplaced optimism which I then expressed. The substitution of the clergy for the Zemstvo in the management of the schools, which less than a year ago I believed to be morally impossible, was effected by the law of June 12, 1884, abolishing the School Councils and transferring all their powers to the bishops and their nominees among the clergy.

If the result of this measure be not to throw back the peasantry into their anti-emancipation condition when, as one of our writers has said, you might travel a week without meeting a *moujik* who could sign his name, it will be because the *moujiks* themselves have acquired a taste for knowledge. As for the Minister of Instruction, we must do him the justice to acknowledge that he has now done everything that man can do to realize the golden dream of despotism—complete ignorance.

CHAPTER XXIX.

THE ZEMSTVO.

I.

THE principle of self-government is no novelty in Russia. When the Muscovite despotism crushed every class under its leaden weight and deprived the people of their most sacred rights, men and citizens, as Mr. Kostomaroff says, protested after their fashion. They indemnified themselves by putting their hands on everything confided to them by the State. To cheat Government, take its money, sell the justice which they dispensed in its name, and pillage the provinces they were charged to administer, became among the public functionaries of ancient Muscovy an accepted, inveterate, and hereditary custom. From the highest to the lowest, everybody stole. They made no distinction between theft and remuneration, robbery and profit. The Central Government itself did not oppose these practices or principles; they only protected against peculation and exaction when, as sometimes happened, the plunderers went to extravagant lengths. A poor boyard, on asking the Tzar for the post of *voevoda*, made no attempt to disguise his motives, generally putting his request in some such terms as these: "Voevoda—— has had his place long enough to grow rich, and I, thy faithful slave, am reduced to beggary, and my servants perish under the sticks of tax-gatherers. Give me, then, this place that I may feed myself a little."

To "give food," or "receive food," was the accepted euphemism to designate nomination to the governorship of a province, a city, or a fortress. In course of time the phrase became obsolete, but until very lately the idea still survived. When the Grand Duke Michael Paolovitch (brother of Tzar Nicolas) was told that Mr. Anisimoff, the colonel of a regiment of guards, had handed over to the regimental fund a sum of 30,000 roubles, saved out of his allowance for supplies, his Highness exclaimed angrily, "It was not to pick up crumbs that a regiment was given him." *

But the appetites of the locusts who were sent into the provinces to fatten, "growing by what they fed on," became so insatiable that the Central Govern-

---

* *Historical Messenger*, December, 1884.

ment, even at a very early date, began to take alarm—the residue left for purposes of State was so little. The check exercised by the *prikases*—chambers composed of Muscovite functionaries (*dyaki*), and themselves as great thieves as the *voevodas*—was quite illusory, and the Government was constrained to call into existence local institutions for protection against the depredations of their own agents.

The first attempt to organize a system of local self-government was made in the reign of Tzar John IV.

In the first part of the St. Petersburg period of the Russian Empire (the reign of Peter the Great), no further attempt to introduce self-government was possible, all the valid forces of the country being engaged in the service of the State. But when a century of progress had produced an educated class the attempt was renewed, taking shape in the so-called Franchise Charter of the Nobility, granted by Catharine II. By this instrument the Empress conferred on the provincial nobility, in meeting assembled, the right of nominating some of the agents of the local administration and the magistracy; the right of controlling all Government functionaries, including the governor-general of the province himself, who had to lay before a commission of the nobility the financial results of his administration.

In seeming, at least, nothing could well be more

complete than the right of control, especially as touching the provincial budget. Yet this function could never be more than a formality; for seigneurs living amidst hordes of slaves it would have been the height of folly to quarrel about a few thousand roubles belonging to the "Crown mother," with the governor of the province and supreme commander of the military forces, which alone held in check the multitude of serfs who cultivated their estates. The new system of aristocratic self-government was a lifeless institution from its very inception, and utterly incapable of defending the State from the colossal depredations of its *tchinovniks*. It was rightly said after the Crimean war that the enemies who had vanquished the armies of Russia were not the allied forces, but her own administrators, furnishers, and functionaries.

When at the conclusion of that contest a general reorganization of the national institutions was found needful, the one essential element for partially safeguarding the State from the immeasurable voracity of its *employés* could not be overlooked. To this end some sort of local representative government was clearly indispensable. Hence, next to the emancipation of the serfs, the most pressing reform was that of the Zemstvo, and of all the institutions established or reformed during the first years of the second Alexander's reign none has suffered relatively so little from the subsequent ferocious reaction as the new Zemstvo.

II.

The decision being taken to establish a system of local self-government as an absolute necessity, a measure to this effect was introduced in 1864. But care was taken not to administer it in too large a dose, the more especially as reactionary views were already beginning to prevail. The part assigned to the Zemstvo in local affairs was, in effect, very limited. They could only deal with twenty-two millions (roubles) of the provincial revenues, and out of this sum they had to support a variety of heavy extraneous charges —keep barracks in repair, feed soldiers, pay the cost of military conscriptions, subsidize the imperial posts, and meet other demands of the same sort. These requirements, which had nothing to do with local government, absorbed the lion's share of the local revenues, and left the Zemstvo only four millions for purposes within their own discretion, and in which they had any direct interest—schools, sanitation, economic enterprises, and so forth. It was not much, and if the Zemstvo were to do any good at all it could hardly have been less.

This restriction was due to a desire to hinder the Zemstvo from displaying too much activity in the domain of finance. To prevent them from trespassing on the domain of politics measures equally efficacious were taken.

Their sessions were very short, and held at long intervals. The deputies could meet only once a year— the district Zemstvo sitting for a fortnight, the provincial Zemstvo three weeks. This scarcely afforded them time to discuss general questions and give their instructions to the *uprava*, an executive commission appointed by each Zemstvo to look after matters in the intervals between their sessions.

In some particulars, indeed, the system of self-government organized in 1864 was inferior to the aristocratic charter of Catharine II. So far from controlling the governor-general, the governor-general controls them, and in the most absolute manner. He audits their accounts, and without his permission the proceedings and discussions of the Zemstvo cannot be made public. He can intervene at any moment and suspend by a word any measure which, in his opinion, is "not in conformity with the general interests and utility of the State," that is to say, which does not precisely please him. True, this veto is merely suspensory, and the Zemstvo may appeal against it to the senate; but as the local parliaments meet only once a year, a resolution tabooed by a governor cannot, in any event, be put in force for a twelvemonth—even if the senate should reverse his decision at once, and not keep the matter in suspense two or three years. In questions of local administration which do not admit of delay, the governor's veto is practically absolute.

To render the dependence of the Zemstvo on the Government still more complete they were deprived of a right formerly enjoyed by their predecessors of the nobility. They could not appoint the chiefs of the inferior administration (*ispravnik*), the right of appointment being vested in the governors. The Zemstvo, moreover, have no executive agents. Whatever they want done must be done by agents of the Government, who give them much trouble, particularly in anything which concerns finance. The collection of the taxes assigned to the Zemstvo, being for the agents of the Imperial Treasury only a secondary service, and, so to speak, a work of complaisance and supererogation, is badly done. The sums due from public properties as well as from great landowners remain outstanding, and arrears accumulate in all directions, to the great annoyance and inconvenience of the Zemstvo.

But to return to the subject more especially before us—the precautions taken to prevent the Zemstvo from meddling with politics. One of these precautions is the denial to them of the right—if so modest a privilege can be called a right—of petitioning the Tzar, a right fully enjoyed by the assemblies of nobles. They are not allowed, in fact, to take the initiative in any question of public utility whatever. They cannot make their voices heard anywhere but in waiting-rooms of the Minister, who is their master, and nine times out of ten does not deign to honour them with a reply.

But the new system of self-government, whatever may be its faults, had one incomparable advantage over the old system—it was not a fraud. The law of emancipation destroyed slavery. It made nobles and peasants fellow-citizens of the same country and equal before the law. It was impossible to limit self-government to a single class; that would have been to revive the old thraldom in a new shape. All classes had thus their allotted part, albeit the division was flagrantly unequal.

The deputies of the Zemstvo are chosen by the order which they represent. The peasants, the towns, and the nobility, elect their representatives separately in separate electoral meetings, which differ somewhat in their composition. The number of the deputies of each order is a fixed quantity, and nothing can be more unfair than the arrangement for the distribution of seats, which is all in favour of the nobility. The peasants, who count sixty millions and pay 83 per cent. of the taxes (90 per cent. according to the calculations of Prince Vassiltchekoff) are represented, in the mean, by 38·6 per cent. of the total number of deputies. The landowning class, numbering only a million individuals and contributing only 7 per cent. to the national revenue, elect 46·2 per cent. of the members of the Zemstvo, while the share of the third estate—the towns—is 15·2 per cent.

In many provinces—the eight central provinces, for instance—the anomaly is still greater; 93,000 great landowners being represented by 1817 deputies, while six million peasants are represented by only 1597.

On the whole, therefore, the nobility hold nearly one-half of the seats in our local parliaments. But this proportion is far from being the measure of their influence, especially in the provincial Zemstvo, where the election is double. The village ancients, who for the most part represent the peasants, are administratively subordinate to the Marshal of the Nobility, who is both chief of the bureau which regulates rural affairs and president of the Zemstvo.

And, finally, in order to exclude from the body the more democratic element of the smaller landowners —the little nobility—the electoral qualification was made inordinately high — the possession of from two to three hundred acres in thickly populated districts, and of eight hundred in localities more sparsely peopled. By this expedient the number of voters belonging to the more highly educated of the aristocratic class is kept very low; they are rather a *coterie* of personal friends and acquaintances than a body of electors.

In point of fact, therefore, the self-governing scheme of 1864 placed the nation under the tutelage of the privileged class, or, more correctly, under the richer and more conservative of that class, to the exclusion of its more liberal and progressive element, the inferior nobility. It is difficult to imagine how Mr. Valoueff could have devised anything less liberal, or more capable of converting self-government into an instrument of reaction and an obstacle to reform. But the Government, after all, was out in its calculations. The occasions on which the aristocratic members of the Zemstvo have tried to turn their power to the profit of the privileged order to which they belong may be counted on the fingers of the two hands. One of the first proceedings of the Zemstvo was an earnest effort to give more power to the peasants, an effort that the Government, which is always proclaiming its partiality for the tillers of the soil, of course opposed. And when at a later date (1871) the Government asked the Zemstvo of the thirty-four provinces for their advice concerning certain changes in the incidence of taxation, all the thirty-four pronounced for the abolition of privilege, advocated a lightening of the heavy charges laid on the peasantry, and recommended the adoption of a scale of taxes proportioned to the means of those on whom they were imposed.

Our Zemstvo, on the other hand, are open to the reproach of an excessive deference to authority and a want of civic courage. The political theories of those of their leaders who have had the boldness to expound them in papers and pamphlets, printed abroad, are far from being models of political wisdom. Their projects of economic reform which have been allowed to see the light are the merest palliatives. I have no desire to sound the praises of our local parliaments. But nobody can deny that they have shown a praiseworthy activity, or that, at the beginning of their career, before the administration laid its hands on their throats, the Russian Zemstvo laboured with all zeal and devotion for the good of the people, and not for the benefit of the class to which the majority of them belonged. Within a few years they increased the local revenues from four to sixteen million roubles, displaying also in other respects a thorough knowledge of the real needs of the country; and the measures they adopted proved them to be possessed of sound sense and practical views. This they showed by taking so much to heart, and at once, the question which is above all others and on which everything else depends — popular instruction, whereby alone the masses can be rendered capable of judging and acting for themselves. We have seen how energetically they wrought to organize primary schools, and how strenuously they defended their work against the attacks of the Minister of Instruction. But the Zemstvo did not limit themselves to the organization of primary education. They tried to create secondary and professional schools so as to bring within reach of the masses technical instruction and a knowledge of practical science. They desired to co-operate with private effort—of which instances are frequent in Russia—in the foundation and endowment of educational institutions of this class, and did space permit I could adduce many other proofs of the energy and enterprise of our local parliaments. They have done everything, in fact, that with their limited resources it was possible to do. The Zemstvo were the first to give to the peasantry some sort of medical care, with which, up to that time, they had been no better provided than African savages. They engaged doctors for country districts, giving the preference to women and competent dispensers. Where they could they built hospitals. They did all in their power, too, to aid economic enterprises which promised to better the wretched lot of the peasantry. The cooperative cheese factories of Vereshaghin, the cooperative industrial enterprises of Shapiro, and many other similar undertakings, received from them generous encouragement and substantial support. Among other good works the Zemstvo founded rural banks, in the hope—unfortunately only in part realized—that, by making loans to the peasants at easy rates of interest, they might be rendered independent of blood-sucking usurers. They advanced money for the purchase by the peasantry of small allotments of land, and introduced the practice of fire assurance. They made every effort to protect the rural population from intimidation on the part of the inferior agents of the administration at election times; to safeguard their home-life from the meddlesomeness of the civil *ouriadnik*, an inferior order of policeman, yet with extensive powers; and their souls from the spiritual *ouriadnik*, the pope—the priest-chicaner and informer, who is continually appealing to the police for aid in restraining his flock from lapsing into heresy and schism.

In all this useful yet moderate activity the greatest obstacles encountered by the Zemstvo were the indolence of office and the open ill-will of the administration. To secure passable dispensers, special schools were necessary, a project which at once roused the spectre of propagandism; and in October, 1866, a law was passed making appointments of dispensers by the Zemstvo contingent on the approval of the governors-general. If it were a question of buying a large lot of seignorial land, there was always some zealot of order to decry the proceeding as part of a confiscatory scheme for the benefit of the peasants and the subversion of the existing *régime*. If it were a question of making head against plagues of locusts and other insectivorous depredators, and enlisting in the work the combined Zemstvo of an infected district, the matter would be allowed to drag on for months, for years even, before the necessary authorization could be obtained—so great is the dread of Government that if once the Zemstvo of several provinces come together they will take to political discussion.

Despite obstacles, however, the Zemstvo made a beginning in all these things; and if they have not been able to do anything great, if they have not succeeded in providing the peasants with good schools and efficient doctors, nor in arresting the progressive impoverishment of the masses, the fault is certainly attributable neither to want of will nor lack of capacity and business aptitude, but to the narrowness of their field of action, and the severity of the restrictions imposed upon them by the State, restrictions which, from the very inception of local self-government, have been gradually intensified and increased.

III.

M. Leroy Beaulieu, in his chapter on the Zemstvo, graphically describes, from his own personal observation, the enthusiasm with which the decree of 1864 for the organization of local parliaments was received by the Russian people. Next to the emancipation of the serfs, there was no reform which gave so much satisfaction and kindled so many hopes as the establishment of the Zemstvo. The learned French writer is, however, mistaken in saying that Russians, in the fervour of their excitement, overlooked the shortcomings of the new measure. A reference to the democratic papers of the time is sufficient to show that the more advanced party of society were fully alive to its serious and manifold defects. And if the bulk of the lettered public, little conversant with practical questions, overrated the merits of the measure, the men of the Zemstvo—the *Zemzy* themselves—were far from sharing in their illusion.

In and about the year 1860, the delegates of the nobility, who afterwards furnished the largest contingent to the Zemstvo — including those of St. Petersburg—expressed on several occasions, in their addresses and petitions, a desire for a measure of local self-government much more extensive and efficient than that which, four years later, was granted. These men, it may be supposed, could not possibly be blind to the true character of the reform of 1864, yet they, of all other people, were the most deceived as to its true character and probable results.

The readiness of a certain class of Russians to be "thankful for small mercies," and welcome with joy concessions which a man of the West would simply despise, is a noteworthy feature of the national character, contrasting curiously with the reverse tendency of another party towards absolute Utopianism—a party which desires to change everything radically and at once, as by the stroke of a wizard's wand, without granting the least indulgence to this decrepit old world, or considering its wants, weaknesses, and long-confirmed habits.

"One of the anomalies of Russian life," is the stereotyped explanation of this phenomenon. But do not these flagrant contrasts all arise from the same source—the ardent desire, now latent, now acute, to do something for the welfare of the people which is seething at the present time in the conscience of instructed Russia? And the lions that stand in the way may surely be vanquished by courage and devotion. There have been dreamers in Russia who hoped to metamorphose the country by means of schools, model farms, and mutual help societies, just as there have been socialist visionaries who hoped to bring back the age of gold by the magic of a revolutionary propaganda.

This faculty for dreaming, which renders people unfit to appreciate hard facts and deal with the things of this world, has greatly impeded social and political progress. Perhaps the time may come when it will prove a blessing. The future will show. In the meantime we have to note a striking example of its baneful results—the creation of a party which in absurdity and self-illusion does not yield even to the Slavophilism of Aksakoff and Khomiakoff—the party, once sufficiently numerous, of which the old Slavophile, Kosheleff, was the leading spirit, and whose fundamental idea was a combination of representative government below with autocracy above. As well try to unite fire and water, or keep iron hot in fresh fallen snow.

The Zemstvo is not a rural commune. It cannot, like the *mir*, sequester itself in its microscopic world, happy if only left in peace. A Zemstvo represents a province, often half as large as Spain, and with a population equal to that of Wurtemberg or Denmark. A thousand interests concern it, a thousand ties unite it with neighbouring provinces. At every step the Zemstvo come in contact with agents of the State. Having to deal with a twentieth part of the provincial revenues, they cannot regard with indifference the stupidity and ingrained incapacity of the *tchinovniks*, who dispose of the remaining nineteen-twentieths. The wish to restrain the bureaucracy, to deprive them more and more of the management of public affairs, is inherent in any system of representative government. The greater the zeal of the Zemstvo for the common weal, the greater must be their desire to lessen still further the power of officialism, beginning with provincial administration, going on to regional business, to finish by controlling and managing the State itself. Political re-organization, representative institutions on the European model, are the ends towards which self-government as inevitably tends as a round stone rolls down an inclined plane, and whatever may be the ideas of Mr. Kosheleff and the Slavophilised *Zemzy*, nothing can arrest its course.

This the Central Government, being a government of *tchinovniks*, have always fully understood; and the Zemstvo, as other Russian representative bodies have done, take frequent occasion to make the administration acquainted with their views. In 1860, and again in 1862, the Assembly of Nobles openly expressed their desire for constitutional reform. The dispersion of the Assembly of St. Petersburg—one of the boldest in the land—and the exile of the principal leaders of the nobility of Tver, are further instances in point. But it is unfortunately a habit of Russian citizens to wait for favourable opportunities for expressing their opinions, instead of making them. The nobility waited for the advent to power of Loris Melikoff to offer some protest, and the St. Petersburg Assembly alone had the hardihood to applaud the frankly liberal speech of Mr. Platonoff,* Marshal of the Nobility of Zarskoi Selo, when he demanded representative institutions and constitutional guarantees for the entire body of citizens. Yet, after all, they had not the courage to signify their approval of the speech by a formal resolution.

The Zemstvo showed more courage, though by no means too much. They have frequently expressed, under divers pretexts, their constitutional aspirations. Sometimes an appeal from the Government to society for help in the contest with terrorism has afforded the opportunity; sometimes it has been found in the presentation of an address to the Emperor after an attempt on his life; or perhaps in a request from the Government for information or advice touching some proposed local measure. Copies of these documents may be found either in the censured or the clandestine Press. According to the organ of the Zemstvo, edited by MM. Kosheleff and

---

* See on this point M. Leroy Beaulieu, vol. ii.

Skalon, there have been presented to the Government since the beginning of the revolutionary period fifteen addresses demanding constitutional reform—three in 1878–79, twelve in 1881. During the existence of the Commission of Experts the greater part of the Zemstvo expressed their desire for a Constituent Assembly, representative of the entire country. The majority of these declarations are expressed in obscure and indirect terms, bordering sometimes on servility. Too often these worthy gentlemen of the Zemstvo, intent on pleasing the police-ridden government, describe the liberty of the future as the faithful servant of the Third Section, and hold before it the attractive perspective of a common crusade against sedition—the very same sedition to which they owed it that the Government at one time besought their help. But happily not all the Zemstvo hold the same language. Russia will always remember with respect the names of Noudatoff and Jdanoff of Samara, Petrounkevitch of Tchernigoff, Netchaeff of Novgorod, Vinberg of Taurida, Gordienko of Kharkoff, and others who have had the courage of their opinions and, in some instances, paid for their temerity with long terms of exile.

I make no citations from these addresses and speeches; English readers would find them modest enough in all conscience. I will merely add that in

Russia they have a more than ordinary significance. They display civic courage for which, unhappily, Russians in general are not distinguished. Everybody knows that for every speech like that of M. Noudatoff, and for every address like that of the Tchernigoff Zemstvo, there are ten which remain inarticulate—hidden *in petto*—and that if they are not proclaimed the reason is easily understood.

IV.

The Government understands and has always understood this. It is not deceived as to the real sentiments of the Zemstvo. The Zemstvo is its natural enemy. The bureaucracy hate it all the more that they are powerless to destroy it, and feel instinctively that sooner or later—if not to-day, then to-morrow—they will have to yield it precedence.

There is nothing surprising in the fact that, when the forces of reaction began to gain ground, the bureaucracy should devise measures for keeping the enemy in check, for preventing the possibility of the Zemstvo taking root in the sphere of its activity, or acquiring a moral influence over public opinion, or uniting together and making combined manifestations and protests against the Government.

But as the Zemstvo were established in 1864 and the extreme reaction began in 1866, it is evident that our young representative institutions have had a hard life. Let me enumerate some of the principal laws—all of them premeditated strokes—which, since that time, have been launched against the Zemstvo. The first affected the most vital principle of public finance. The Regulation of 1864 conferred on the Zemstvo the right of levying taxes. But to impose additional burdens on the already overcharged peasants was extremely difficult and painful for an institution whose chief aim was to better the peasants' condition. It was an expedient, moreover, not likely to be very productive. The only means of ensuring financial prosperity was for the Zemstvo to find new sources of revenue. They thought they had found them in charges on industrial undertakings. Nothing could have been wiser or more just, and the Zemstvo prospered accordingly. Yet the taxes they imposed on industry were very light compared with those imposed on agriculture. In some provinces industry paid on a scale equal to an income tax of two roubles per thousand, while agriculture paid eleven and a half times as much. But it was not long before Government came to the rescue of the privileged, and by the law of November 19, 1866, put an end to the equitable and successful system of finance which the Zemstvo had introduced.

The famous measure in question interdicted absolutely the levying of taxes on the capital or profits of industrial enterprises. As a set-off the Zemstvo were allowed to put an insignificant duty on trade certificates, and lay a trifling rate on factory buildings. This was to re-establish an unjust exemption and virtually ruin the Zemstvo. The law of November 19th was looked upon by the friends of the institution as indirectly involving the destruction of local parliaments, and deliberately designed to render them both powerless and unpopular. So heavy was the blow that over half the Zemstvo joined in a chorus of protests. The Government retaliated by dissolving the Zemstvo of St. Petersburg, whereupon all the others laid down their arms.

The year following—seven months later—came the law of June 13th, which sapped the Zemstvo on the side of their political importance. No longer content with controlling them through the provincial governors, the Government resolved to have an agent in the very heart of the citadel. The chairman of the Zemstvo ceased to be a mere director of debates. He became at once president and chief. The Minister nominated him, and only the Minister can depose him. He is a mere *tchinovnik* whom the new law empowers to interrupt any speech at discretion, or stop any motion, discussion, or resolution which in his opinion might give umbrage to the Government.

Between these two laws—one of the economic order, the other of the political order—the Zemstvo were held as in a vice. The other prescriptions concern only matters of secondary importance. By the Regulations of 1864 the different Zemstvo could, in cases of emergency, enter into communications with each other, always provided, of course, that the Government did not object. But on May 4, 1867, there appeared an "instruction" which explained that this clause must be construed in a strictly Pickwickian sense—that the Zemstvo would not be allowed to communicate with each other in any case, let it be as urgent as it might. The stringency of the Government on this point was so excessive that, when a plague broke out in Astrakan and the local Zemstvo asked leave to confer with the Zemstvo of neighbouring provinces as to the best means of meeting the emergency, the request was refused.

The "instruction" as to the printing of the Zemstvo's accounts and the reports of their proceedings may also be noted as a curiosity of Russian administration. It explained that these reports might indeed be printed, but only as many copies were to be issued, as there were members of the Zemstvo—not one more.

It is evident that with a code of laws like these, to which must be added the right exercised by the Government of arresting and exiling any deputy whom it may dislike or mistrust, the utility of our local parliaments is attenuated almost to nothingness. In these circumstances it is not surprising that the public should have lost all interest in an institution which at the outset they so enthusiastically acclaimed. The best men have withdrawn altogether from the Zemstvo, and are too often succeeded by intriguers and self-seekers. Members are slack in their attendance, and it not unfrequently happens that a session cannot be held for want of a quorum. The discussions have degenerated into formalities. Nobody takes an interest in them, for all know that any proposal for the benefit of the people will be tabooed by the Government. The Zemstvo simply vegetate in sordid abandonment.

But they still exist in a fashion, and serve as a framework capable of being filled up at any moment with solid material; and, should a crisis come to pass, the Zemstvo may exercise a decisive influence. The Government fears them, and would gladly destroy them utterly. The celebrated commission under the presidency of General Kakhanoff, the little Lykurgus of the reaction, proposed so to raise the voting qualification that the suffrage would be restricted to the largest landowners, who were among the most inveterate of the anti-abolitionists. This, as Russian papers have rightly said, would be to reestablish the bureaucratic system in all its purity. It would not even be an oligarchy, for Russia possesses no aristocracy in the true sense of the word. Count Tolstoi's oligarchic dreams are no less absurd than the clerical dreams of his worthy colleague, Pobedonostzeff. Our great landowners, who spend their lives in the capital, occupying nearly always places in the administration, are an element altogether heterogeneous and strange in the localities to which they belong.

Not desiring to repeat the penance I have had to perform for my incredulity as to turning over to the clergy the direction of primary education, I refrain from saying that the project in question is impossible. The reaction has become so reckless that it is ready to attempt even the impossible. I will say only that, in view of the general impoverishment of the country, the definitive abolition of the Zemstvo (or a measure equivalent to its abolition) would have the most disastrous effects, and might not improbably be the precursor of national bankruptcy.

"If anybody would know the incapacity of our bureaucracy to administer any public affairs whatever," wrote an old member of the Zemstvo, in a pamphlet printed not very long ago,* "I would recommend him to study the papers published by the earlier Zemstvo on the state in which they found the interests confided to their charge. According to these reports, especially when read between the lines, the condition of the country could hardly have been worse if it had just been ravaged by foreign invaders. Instead of stores of grain the Zemstvo found in one place only empty barracks; in another they found no trace of a school whatever, although it was entered in the reports of the *tchinovniks* as possessing several schools, for the maintenance of which they had received yearly money grants. In another, again, had disappeared a bridge, nobody knew exactly when, which for years past had required periodical repairs. In still another locality the same fate had befallen an hospital. The report of the commission of the Zemstvo of Perm thus describes the state of affairs when they first took them in hand: 'We examined the public granaries. One was quite empty; in the other we saw only a number of boxes gnawed by rats. On inquiry we were told that they contained the confiscated property of some sectaries. We opened them. Instead of property they contained only rat nests. Of the corn

---

* S. Z., "The Eighteen Years' Struggle between the Bureaucracy and the Zemstvo." Geneva.

entered as being in store there was not a grain. The funds assigned for supplies existed only on paper; those for agricultural subsidies the same. For medical purposes the same, and where hospitals existed they were in such a state that the people fled from them as if they were slaughter-houses '" (pp. 3 and 4).

I leave the reader to judge for himself what state the finances of Russia are likely to be in when the provinces relapse into their former condition.

CHAPTER XXX.

THE DESPOTISM AND THE PRESS.

I.

IF anybody required a thermometer of great sensitiveness, showing at every period and every moment the variation in the intensity of Russian despotism, he would find it in the position of the Press. "The liberty of the Press is the chief guarantee of the liberty of a country," said Milton. With equal reason we may affirm the opposite—the existence of a despotism depends on the fettering of the Press. Despotic governments understand this. There is no department of human activity which despots regard with so much suspicion as the Press. In Russia, as we have seen, the Government has not too much love for schools any more than for local parliaments; but the Press is in much worse case than either of them. Self-government and schools bring forth their fruits in a time more or less distant; the Press acts immediately. The domains of the schools and the Zemstvo are limited; the Press commands the whole extent of the empire. In every other field of action the adversary is always an individual; professors, members of the Zemstvo, and the rest, however disagreeable they may be, are at least people, men, known personalities. But a writer, what is he? Perhaps a monster without law and without faith, capable of anything. To what purpose may he not turn that mysterious power which by virtue of his venomous pen he wields over the weak and foolish?

On the other hand, no human institution is naturally so defenceless as the Press. In all others thought and spirit are more or less intimately allied with matter. Self-government and instruction are necessary for the State itself, for its efficient working and its material well-being. But of the Press the State has no need. True it has recourse to the printer for the preparation of its official publications; but that is not the Press. The veritable Press, the brain of the nation, despotism can well spare and still live, just as certain animals can survive for a long time the loss of a cerebral lobe. The Press, so to speak, is sublimated thought, and incapable of self-defence. It is the duty of the other members of the social body to unite for the protection of this vital part of the organism; if they are incapable of doing this the Press is at the mercy of Power. The Government holds it in its grasp, and can either crush the victim to death or let it live and breathe according to its good pleasure.

The position of the Press is thus an excellent thermometer for measuring at every moment the intensity of despotism. From this point of view the history of the relations of the Russian Press and the Russian Government is highly interesting.

Russia has never known anything which remotely resembles the liberty of the Press or tolerance for political and religious ideas. Peter the Great, whose reign was the apogee of imperial liberalism, tortured and put to death the sectarian writers who wrote pamphlets against his reforms. But the Tzar was all in favour of European culture, and everything savouring thereof passed the frontier without inspection. It is told that when the translator of Puffendorf's "Universal History" proposed to omit some passages not too complimentary to Muscovy, Peter gave him a little paternal correction with his famous cane, for showing so little respect for the great historian, and ordered the scribe to print the passage just as it was. Peter's immediate successors followed his example. They protected letters and science, made *mezenots*, founded academies, and established literary journals. Catharine II. posed as a literary character, wrote with her own hand moral tales and insipid novels "with a purpose," and deigned to plagiarize Shakespeare's "Merry Wives of Windsor." True, the censorship existed at that time, but it was not the heterogeneous body of *tchinovniks*, instinctively hostile to authors and letters, which it has since become. Savants and professors censured the works of other savants and professors, younger or less distinguished than themselves. And, curiously enough, the animosities and jealousies of the writers of that epoch were more inimical to the freedom of the Press than the despotism itself. Scabitchevsky, in his history of the censorship in Russia, relates that when the *Academic Journal* was published without being submitted to the censors, the writers of that day, like the lackeys that they were, mutually denounced each other, and lauded the censorship as an institution of the highest value. The Government, on their part, vainly tried to make these angry scribes listen to reason, exhorting them to be more tolerant, and showing them that the world would not come to an end even if people were allowed the free expression of their opinions.

It would be a mistake to attribute the patriarchal relations which prevailed between the tzars and the tzarinas and the writers of this period, either to the liberalism of the former or the docility of the latter. The cause was much more simple.

The reforms of Peter the Great had brought Russia into temporary unison with the rest of Continental Europe, and at that time the autocracies of the Continent were bureaucratic autocracies like that of Russia. So long as this unison existed the science, laws, and histories of neighbouring nations could present no danger. In what respect could they be dangerous? An occasional sarcastic reference to Muscovite barbarism, like that of Puffendorf, there might be; but nothing serious, nothing to imperil the bases of order. True, in the eighteenth century there was a vast philosophic movement in Europe, which contained the germs of a great political reform. But as yet these germs had not shown themselves. They were hidden under the mask of humanitarianism and philosophy. Princes associated themselves with the movement, thinking they would be able to dominate and direct it. And our Catharine II., like Frederick the Great, was a philosopher and paid court to Voltaire.

The revolution changed all this then and for ever. As touching its political institutions and its culture Europe made a great step in advance. Russia remained what Peter had made her. Then began the persecutions. Radisheff and Novikoff were the two first martyrs of the Russian Press. The one was exiled to Siberia, the other imprisoned, for the advocacy of ideas which Catharine, before the revolution, had herself professed. The mutual positions of the Government and the Press were then distinctly defined. Since that time the persecutions may have varied in intensity, but they have never been intermitted.

How Nicolas dealt with authors and journalists is known to all students of contemporary history. In the time of Alexander the Press was the first institution to feel the weight of his hand. The elder Kosheleff, in his posthumous memoirs, tells how in 1858, in the very honeymoon of Alexander's liberalism, when the Tzar, supported by the flower of the nation, was waging war against the obscurantism of the old nobility for the emancipation of the serfs, the persecution of the censorship reduced him to despair and ruined the paper edited by the Slavophile, Aksakoff, and himself. This although the journal in question was an ardent advocate of emancipation and its two editors were inveterate monarchists! Despotism will tolerate no criticism, even from its partisans. The condemnation of Mikailoff and Schapoff and the moral ruin of Tchernychevsky, men of the greatest intelligence Russia ever possessed, were also the work of the first period of Alexander's reign.

Sometimes waxing, at others waning, according to changes of the wind in high quarters, the persecution of the Press went on without surcease the whole of the twenty-six years during which the late Tzar swayed the destinies of his country.

II.

But it is with the actual condition of the Press, not with the past persecutions of poets, novelists, historians, and journalists, that we have to deal. And here, at the outset, it is well to notice a significant and characteristic fact—that whenever the Government are constrained by financial requirements or political necessity to concede some measure of reform the Press is the last to profit by the change. When the emancipation of the serfs, the organization of the Zemstvo, and the establishment of the New Courts lent to the life of the country another aspect and gave promise of a better and a brighter future, the Press, whose duty it is to animate, to enlighten, and to encourage, was still left to the tender mercies of the ancient censorship. Not until 1865 was the new Press Law promulgated, and even then, few as were its concessions, it was granted grudgingly and ungraciously. The Russian Government never hesitates to retrace its steps, or take back with one hand what it gives with the other, and the new law was expressly termed "a provisional regulation." It was an experiment which could be discontinued at any moment that might be deemed expedient. Its application was, moreover, restricted in a manner altogether exceptional. New laws, if they make for more liberty, are rarely applicable to the whole of the empire. Thus the Zemstvo, the justices of the peace, and the new Courts were instituted gradually, as if the authorities were afraid of disgusting the country with too much freedom ; and the process has been so cautiously conducted that there are still districts where the reforms in question have not even yet come into operation. But, as touching the new Press Law, the authorities surpassed themselves ; not content with making the regulation provisional, they limited its application strictly to the two capitals. It is true that the Government officially undertook to extend the enactment to the provinces so soon as the new tribunals were completely organized ; but the promise was never fulfilled, and the whole of Russia outside Moscow and St. Petersburg still remains under the domination of the old Press Law of Nicolas I.

Let us see what were the character and extent of the concessions which the Government so timidly and so reluctantly granted. The new law substituted the correctional for the preventive censorship ; but, as touching works with less than ten sheets of original matter, or twenty sheets of translation, the old system was retained. Periodical publications in existence at the date of publication of the new regulation might, if their proprietors desired it, enjoy the privilege of the correctional censure. Afterwards, however, it could be obtained by a special authorization granted by the Minister.

Yet, although preventive censorship was abolished, measures were taken to hinder the privilege from being abused. It was ordered that, after an edition had been printed, and before it was sent out for sale, a copy of the book should be submitted to the Committee of Censors, nominated by the Minister — a body which had power to forbid being delivered to the publishers any work they might deem dangerous to loyalty, morality, or religion. As for newspapers and other similar publications, the law authorized the Minister, at his discretion, to warn officially any journal of the views or statements to which he might take exception. A third warning entailed, *ipso facto*, the offending paper's suspension and the prosecution of its conductors. The Minister may, moreover, by administrative order, which means by the simple exercise of his will, suspend any journal whatever for from three to six months. He has further the right to stop the sale of any paper in the kiosques and by newsboys in the streets—that is to say, he may cut off half its sale at a stroke; he may also forbid it to publish advertisements. These two measures, when enforced against any journal so unfortunate as to incur the Minister's displeasure, are tantamount to the infliction of a heavy fine, which, if repeated, it is impossible for the victim to survive, there being practically no limit to the amount of the penalty the Government may inflict. This method of crushing an obnoxious journal has of late been frequently practised, for it makes less noise and seems less arbitrary than suspension by administrative order, or even after three warnings.

On the other hand, the law of 1865 possessed one great and positive advantage. The definitive suppression of a book or a newspaper could be pronounced only by the judgment of a court, and though provisional suspension by Government decree or administrative order, or deprivation of its advertisements, might ruin a journal utterly, the mere possibility of an appeal was a decided gain, tending as it did to make the Minister more cautious in the exercise of his powers, and more amenable to public opinion. The appeal could be made in the last resort to the Senate of the Empire—a body not likely to treat revolutionary theories or subversive ideas too leniently, as was sufficiently proved by its condemnation of the journal conducted by Mr. Aksakoff, the Muscovite Slavophile. Nevertheless, the Senate acted always judicially, and, as it showed in the matters of the translation of the first volume of Lecky's "History of Rationalism," and of Youndt's "The Soul of Man and Animals," was able sometimes to check flagrant injustice by reversing the decisions of the Committee of Censors. In cases of urgency, however, the authorities did not scruple to disregard the law which themselves had made. In 1866, hardly a year after its enactment, Prince Gagarine and his friends resolved, by hook or by crook, to effect the suppression of the *Contemporary* of Nekrasoff and the *Russian Word* of Blagosvetloff, and they prevailed on the Tzar to act as their *deus ex machinâ*. One evening at a ball His Majesty gave the order in two words for the extinction of the obnoxious journals, and they were suppressed accordingly without any formality whatsoever. But after a while it was deemed expedient to convert the exception into the rule. Trials, even when won by the prosecution, made a noise, excited public opinion, and helped to spread ideas which the administration desired to crush. Despotisms prefer darkness and shade to publicity and light, and in 1872 the law of 1865 was "amended" by a supplementary enactment, depriving the tribunals of the power of intervening in the affairs of the Press, and vesting the control of them in the Council of Ministers, who decide, in the last resort, on the fate of any book or periodical which may be in question, after hearing the report of the Minister of the Interior. Thus the latter, being both accuser and judge—for his colleagues, in matters that concern his department, must necessarily adopt his views—became the supreme arbiter of the Press and purveyor of literature for the entire Russian nation. In 1882 another change was introduced, though, practically, it made no great difference. A committee of four was substituted for the full Ministerial Council, but, as before, no defence was admitted, the committee deliberating and deciding *in camerâ*. Another measure was the application to recalcitrant journals of the preventive censure.

Since 1872 suspensions, suppressions, deprivations of the right to receive advertisements and sell single copies have rained on the unfortunate Russian Press as from a horn of abundance. Books banned by the censors are remorselessly burnt. Thus were condemned to the flames the second volume of Lecky's "History of European Morals" (the first volume was sanctioned), Hobbes's "Leviathan," Haeckel's "History of Creation," Voltaire's "Essai sur les Mœurs," and many more. The same fate has also befallen divers Russian authors, who are treated with so little ceremony that Prougavine's book, entitled "Religious Sects" (albeit the articles composing it had appeared in the periodical form, and, therefore, been passed by the censors), was burnt by order of the Committee of Ministers.

III.

But to gauge rightly the real position of the Russian Press something more is required than mere knowledge of the law as it stands. We must go behind the scenes, because it is there, in the shade, that the despotism shows itself without disguise. When the Minister desires to impose his will on the Press he has recourse to secret *ordonnances*, which end always with the same formula—"In case of disobedience the articles of this or that regulation will be applied to the refractory journal," which means that contempt of the order will entail either suspension or suppression. This proceeding, re-establishing, as in effect it does, the preventive censure under another form, is of course flagrantly illegal, and contrary both to the letter and the spirit of the law. But the despotism of those above is so absolute, the submission of those below so complete, that the representatives of the Press have never been able to join in a protest against the tyranny by which they are so ruthlessly victimized, and the protest of a single journal would expose it to the implacable vengeance of the Government. To give an idea of the character of the *ordonnances* in question, I cite a few specimens which were given in the *Narodnaia Volia* of August, 1883, a clandestine journal being the only medium through which facts of this sort can be made known.

On March 4, 1881, three days after the murder of Alexander II., the Minister sent to the Press a secret *ordonnance* thus conceived: "Several organs of the Press, under the pretext of extraordinary circumstances, have allowed themselves to print articles very indiscreetly suggesting the expediency of reorganizing our political system, and expressing doubts as to the existence of patriotism in the higher circles of our society, which are accused of indifference to the true interests of the nation. The appearance of articles of this character will entail the suppression of the journals in which they may be published."

On March 25th, the department, "considering the near approach of the trial for the abominable crime of March 1st, reminds conductors of journals of the order against printing, under pain of suspension, original accounts of political trials." (The papers were permitted to print only the carefully prepared account of the proceedings given in the Official *Gazette*.)

In April, 1881, there occurred some disorders among university students. On the 16th of the same month the following order was issued: "It is considered necessary to forbid the Press to discuss this matter, to give any news concerning it, or print any communications relating thereto. Disobedience of this *ordonnance*," &c.

The next order I shall cite is very curious and merits particular attention. It was issued on April 29th, " In view of the *coup d'état* which has come to pass in Bulgaria, and considering the necessity of supporting Prince Alexander, the Government is desirous that our Press should speak with circumspection (*sic*) of the events accomplished at Sofia." This order was supplemented by a circular dated May 9th, wherein it is explained that, although the papers are forbidden to censure, they are free to praise the *coup d'état* of General Ernrod. The *ordonnance* was, therefore, in effect, an invitation to the Press to defend an arbitrary and illegal act committed in a foreign country, the object being to make it appear that not alone the Russian Government but Russian society fully approved the proceeding. The explanatory circular was issued because the Press, either out of malice or timidity, construed the order too literally, and made no comment whatever on the incident in question.

The resignation of Loris Melikoff involved, as is well known, the downfall of the moderate Liberal party and the extinction of all hope of reform, a result that excited among all classes of the capital so general a feeling of disappointment and discontent as seriously to annoy the Government, and on May 18th a circular was sent to the papers instructing them to make no mention whatever of "to-day's proceedings in the Municipal Council, or to discuss the proposal to present General Loris Melikoff with the freedom of the city." It was equally forbidden to publish the debates of the Council on this question.

On August 17th of the same year the Press was requested, in the accepted form, to refrain from printing any articles whatever against General Baranoff, former Prefect of St. Petersburg. The general had a short time before distinguished himself by some very original measures for the preservation of order, and by his so-called "Parliament," an institution which excited general ridicule.

The Liberalism which prevailed in the higher circles of the administration during the Melikoff period produced a movement among the Zemstvo that continued after the Minister's dismissal, a fact that sufficiently accounts for a circular issued on May 28th, inviting the journals of the two capitals to abstain from all comment on the "decisions, motions, and addresses" of the Zemstvo and the municipalities.

When Count Ignatieff, the successor of Loris Melikoff, came into office, one of his first proceedings was to appoint numerous commissioners for the elaboration of projects of reform in various branches of the administration. Troubles in the south and outrages against Israelites in other parts of the empire had directed attention to the Jewish question, and a commission was nominated to prepare a report on the subject. It was a question which greatly interested both the public and the Press, and an open discussion of the matter could hardly have failed to facilitate the work of the commission and might have given rise to some valuable suggestions. But the Government, fearing criticism, and haunted as always by the dread of "exciting public opinion" and thereby producing all sorts of terrible consequences, sent out, on May 31, 1881, a circular, "forbidding the publication of articles likely to create discontent with the measures of the Government, which cannot be tolerated, above all at a time so difficult as the present." In other words, the sole alternative of silence was to praise all Government measures without distinction.

A few days later (June 3rd) an *ordonnance* was issued directing the Press to " speak with the greatest circumspection (the reader will understand the meaning of this phrase, so frequently used) of the proceedings of the special commission for reducing the price of the lands acquired by the peasants." On September 19th it was considered necessary to forbid the " publication of any news whatever concerning the report of the special commission on the relations between the indigenous population and the Jews." On October 10, 1881, an interdict was laid on the publication "of any articles whatever on peasant migrations." On January 28, 1882, it was ordained in the usual manner that, " in view of the preparation of reforms in the organization of professional schools," no discussion of the subject shall take place, nor any news about it be published. On March 17th, "it is absolutely forbidden to publish in the papers any news whatever concerning the re-partition of properties, equalization of lots, &c., or any articles suggesting the justice of changes in the economical condition of the peasantry." On April 20th was issued another circular about the Jews forbidding "all reference to the deliberations of the Council of Ministers on the subject, or the publication of any articles whatever on the question in general."

On October 29, 1882, it was forbidden to speak of

the expulsion of the gymnasium pupil, Fougalevitch (of Kamenez Padolsk, who insulted the inspector, but was acquitted by the tribunal). On November 1st a circular was issued inviting the Press to keep silence as to the troubles in the University of Kazan. On December 16th it was forbidden to say anything about the prosecution of the student Semenoff for insulting the Curator of the University. On February 4, 1882, it was forbidden to publish any news concerning the "domestic relations" of the family of Councillor Markus. On November 23rd it was ordered that no mention should be made of the misunderstanding between the Curator Neuhart and Dr. Kwatz. On October 4th was issued the following order: "The foreign Press makes mention of the implication of Count P. A. Valueff in the trial relating to dilapidation of State property in the province of Orenburg. It is forbidden to reproduce this news." Here we have an illustration of the Russian proverb, "One dirty hand washes the other, and both become clean."

But the worst has yet to be told. On June 12th was issued a circular bluntly informing editors that the publication of articles on the relations of peasants to their landlords, or on "the Lutorique affair," would entail the suppression of the journal in which they might appear. On June 26, 1882, the Minister in formed editors that "virulent articles having appeared on the affair of Prince Sherbatoff and his former serfs, and as such articles might have a bad influence on the relations of proprietors and peasants, it is expressly forbidden to speak of the Sherbatoff affair." The two affairs in question related to cruelties inflicted on peasants so horrible that in any other country the perpetrators would have been put on their trial.

Still another fact. The catastrophe of Koukoueff was one of the most heartrending of our national calamities. A train ran off the line and went headlong into a morass. Many of the passengers were badly hurt and more than a hundred killed. The accident, as was fully proved, arose from the unsound condition of the permanent way and the rottenness of the piles, the engineers and managers having appropriated to their own purposes the moneys assigned for repairs. On this becoming known there was a cry of indignation from one end of Russia to the other. And the Government—what course did it take? Promise a searching inquiry and the exemplary punishment of the delinquents? Nothing of the sort. It issued this circular:—"August 19, 1882.—Since the disaster on the Koursk Railway, several papers have printed articles bringing grave charges against some of the *employés* of the Ministry of Roads. Articles of this sort having a disturbing character, their publication will bring on the offending journal the severest administrative penalties." Thus the State forbade parents and friends to protest against the authors of their misfortune, or to offer an opinion on the best method of preventing further similar disasters.

This terminates our record. The samples I have produced are eminently characteristic. They show the tendencies of the Russian Government, and reveal the crooked ways of bureaucratic despotism. The Press is regarded as a hostile and essentially pernicious force, to be partially tolerated only because it cannot be utterly destroyed. The policy of the Ministry towards the Press is dictated by the narrowest official spirit. The moment a question becomes prominent or interesting, its discussion is tabooed. Of publicity, talk, the free expression of thought, the Government stands in mortal dread. Even when it takes some hesitating step in advance, or resolves to attempt this or that reform, its first proceeding is to forbid all discusion of it by the Press. Everything must be done in silence and secrecy and in the back rooms of Ministerial Cabinets. But human thought is not easily fettered. Harassed by proscription, indications, warnings, and admonitions, threatened on the least show of disobedience with a whole arsenal of pains and penalties, opinion takes the weapon of the feeble and meets force with cunning. A secret understanding is established between writers and readers. An esoteric language, made up of allusions, hints, and conventional phrases, is created; and so the ideas which our rulers have banned still pass from mind to mind.

IV.

It is a patent fact that our Press is almost altogether liberal and anti-governmental—or was so while Russia had a Press. This Mr. Katkoff himself does not attempt to deny. The organs of reaction may be counted on the fingers of one hand. Most Russian papers are either frankly liberal or shrewdly artful, alternating between servility, to escape the censure, and opposition, to please their readers. The oppositionist tendencies of the Russian Press on the one hand, and bureaucratic obscurantism on the other, are leading rapidly to a collision which can hardly fail to be fatal to the weaker of the two forces. The history of the struggle between them—if that may be called a struggle in which one party can offer hardly a show of resistance—presents three distinct phases. The provincial Press was the first to suffer. Being under the preventive censure, the administration had only to draw the bonds a little tighter in order to crush it utterly. Less known, having less influence and fewer readers, country papers may be treated with less ceremony than their contemporaries of the two capitals. Altogether, it may be averred without exaggeration that, notwithstanding its lack of literary polish, the part of our Press the most sympathetic, the most devoted to the public weal and capable of promoting national well-being, were our country papers. But the *tchinovniks* of St. Petersburg were not at all disposed to allow free play to their usefulness. The spectre of separatism was summoned against them, and they became the first victims of the reaction. The holocaust went on easily and quietly, without too much scandal, and was all but completed before the death of Alexander II. It required only a word to the censors, and the work was begun. One by one the best country papers, weary of the annoyance, the chicanery, and the oppression to which they were continually exposed, gave up the struggle. Suppression by decree was unnecessary; they were worried out of existence by administrative ordinances, each more impossible and absurd than the other. Purely political papers were ordered strictly to avoid domestic subjects. Journals founded for the express purpose of defending Jewish interests and promoting a fusion of the two races were forbidden to make any allusion to the Jewish question. The expedients of the department were sometimes marked by a grim humour all its own. One was to appoint as special censor of an obnoxious print an official living at the other extremity of the empire. This involved the sending to him of every proof, both of comment and news, before publication. Hence the paper upon which this practical joke was played could not appear until ten or fifteen days after its contemporaries of the same town or district. No journal giving news a fortnight out of date could possibly go on, and journals so treated rarely attempted to reappear. But as nobody could say that the Government had suppressed them, there was neither scandal nor "agitation of spirits;" one more unfortunate had died a natural death—that was all. Were dealt with in this way the *Novotcherkask Don*, the *Kama Gazette*, and the *Tiflis Obzor*. They were ordered to send their proofs, not as usual to the local censors, but to the censor of Moscow, which is distant in time (including the return journey) from Novotcherkask seven days, from Kama ten to twelve, and from Tiflis twenty. The two first made no attempt either to comply with the order or to continue their issues, but Mr. Nicoladze, proprietor of the *Obzor*, in order to preserve the right of publication (which lapses if not used during a year), brings out his paper every January. The *Obzor* is probably the only daily paper in the world which appears once a year.

It would, however, be a mistake to suppose that the department holds to the letter of the law, loose as that is. The expedients I have described seem to be adopted out of a spirit of pure mischief, pretty much as a cat torments a mouse before giving it the *coup de grâce;* for, when the humour takes them, the authorities do not hesitate to suppress by a stroke of the pen a paper which has been submitted to the preventive censure, and is therefore irresponsible to the administration. Thus were suppressed the Kieff *Telegraph*, the Odessa *Pravda*, and the Smolensk *Messenger*. The Tiflis *Phalanga* was suppressed *for presenting to the censor* a drawing which was deemed dangerous and unsuitable for publication! I believe, too, that the Kieff *Troud* has lately shared the same fate. All these were under the preventive *régime*, which means, of course, that they were not allowed to publish a line unseen by the censor. In 1876 the Government, utterly regardless of the law, and without assigning a reason, suppressed an entire literature —that of the Ukraine. Except novels, it was forbidden to publish anything whatever in the language of that country—a proceeding absolutely without precedent even in Russia.

Nearly all these measures were taken in the time of Alexander II. By throwing every possible impediment in the way of starting new journals, by having censors only in a few of the principal towns (which rendered it well-nigh impossible to conduct papers in any other town), the Government found no difficulty in practically extinguishing the provincial Press. Hence Alexander III. had only to do with the Press of the two capitals, and it must be admitted that in this contest Count Ignatieff and, above all, Count Tolstoi showed more discernment than was displayed by our generals in the war against Turkey—they attacked the enemy where he was weakest.

CHAPTER XXXI.

THE PRESS UNDER ALEXANDER II.

I.

Russia, which differs from Western Europe in so many other things, differs also in the relative importance of its periodic publications. Daily papers, being essentially political, cannot in a country without political life wield the same influence as in England, France, and the United States. Popular institutions we have none; public opinion is ignored. There are no questions which depend on the votes of a body of citizens to whom it is necessary to appeal day by day, and whose views may be influenced by argument and explanation. The struggle, so far as it goes, is with us limited to the domain of ideas. But for the discussion and development of ideas newspapers, even if they could always afford the necessary space, are not always the most suitable medium. On this point, moreover, the Russian public is exacting; they demand something more solid and serious than it is possible for daily journals to give. Vital questions, which in free countries are discussed in parliaments, meetings, and clubs, can be treated in Russia only in the Press—so far as the censor may permit. Hence the preponderance in our periodic literature of magazines and reviews, which, while not neglecting the events of the day, give a considerable proportion of their space to the higher subjects of domestic and general interest, sometimes even to standard works of a class that in any other country would be published in separate editions. Works of fiction are confined to monthly publications. Novels of merit appear in the first instance nearly always in reviews as serials, never as *feuilletons* in newspapers. All this gives an exceptional importance to Russian reviews, and in its crusade against the Press the Department, guided and inspired by Ignatieff and Tolstoi, opened the attack, as has already been said, against the enemy's weakest part—the daily newspaper.

In order to form an idea of the damage sustained by Russian journals in this unequal warfare we have only to glance at the *Souvorine's Almanac*, where are recorded all the rigorous measures of which the Press has lately been the victim. Since the beginning of the present reign eight high-class St. Petersburg papers have been either summarily suppressed by administrative order or harassed to death by incessant persecutions. During this time they received forty-eight admonitions, were as often provisionally suspended (for from four weeks to eight months), and suffered incalculable money loss by interdicts to publish advertisements and sell by retail. The daily Press, in fact, has been virtually crushed, for among the defunct journals were some of the most important the country possessed, such as the *Poriadok*, the *Golos*, and others. Only two or three liberal papers of any influence still survive the persecution, dragging on a miserable existence, threatened and badgered at every turn, and expecting that every day will be their last.

The war against the great reviews, which had been resolved upon from the first, albeit the resolution was allowed to remain some time in abeyance, began with the suppression of the *Slovo*. The editor having retired, the Department refused to sanction the appointment of a successor, and in a private interview with the publisher the chief cynically avowed that he would not accept even a declared monarchist. After eight months of resistance, remonstrance, and suspense (during which time the review was not allowed to appear), the proprietor lost all hope, and the *Slovo* was numbered among the slain. Then, after an interval of admonitions which led to no particular result, the Government dropped the mask, and suppressed the *Annals of the Country*. The *Annals* was beyond compare the best review we had. In circulation and in influence, as well as in the quality of its articles and the ability of its contributors, the *Annals* was far ahead of the best of its contemporaries. Its subscribers numbered nearly 10,000—a figure in Russia altogether phenomenal. The *Messenger of Europe*, its strongest competitor, could not boast of a circulation of more than 6000. The tendency of the *Annals* being essentially democratic, it naturally gave much attention to all questions touching on the condition of the people. In this regard it has rendered immense service to the nation; nobody can take a single step in the study of our domestic economy without referring for instruction and information to the back numbers of the *Annals*. Even the members of our unteachable Government, when it is a question of doing something for the toiling millions of the nation, preparing an important financial scheme, or introducing an economic reform, are compelled to go to the same source, as well for their facts as for their ideas. In an article which I contributed to the *Contemporary Review*, when speaking of the blindness of certain writers who contend that Russia is still unfitted to be her own mistress, I observed that the best proof to the contrary lay in the fact that the Russian Government has never adopted, or even submitted to the fruitless consideration of a commission of *tchinovniks*, a single progressive measure which had not been previously indicated, discussed, and put in much better form by the Press and the Zemstvo. Of this the *Annals* affords ample illustration and abundant proof. Mr. Scalon pointed out, and thoroughly discussed in the pages of the review, the insufficiency of the allotments assigned to the peasants, at least ten years before the question was taken up by the Government. Mr. Chaslavsky and Mr. Trirogoff dwelt on the same thing, and called the attention of the authorities to the necessity of the measures. As is well known, when the socialist agitation and the gradual impoverishment of the peasants compelled the Government at length to act, they dealt, however inadequately, with the land question on the lines suggested by the review which they have since suppressed. Reform of the methods of taxation and of the law of settlement was exhaustively discussed in the review long before these questions were submitted for the consideration of Loris Melikoff's and Count Ignatieff's Commissions. The measures adopted to save from total ruin the so-called *chinsceviki*, a sort of perpetual farmer, were due to the articles of Mr. Koteliansky, who was the first to point out their wretched condition, and denounce the injustice to which they were exposed. A still more striking instance of the utility of discussion and the power of the pen is found in the fact that the abolition of the salt duty was brought about in great measure by the efforts of the *Annals*. At the time of Loris Melikoff's advent to power, there appeared in the review a series of articles by Mr. Leonidas Cherniaev, in which he set forth with great force the impolicy of taxing salt, and the manifold hardships which the imposts entailed, and the new dictator, desiring to signalize his accession to office by an act of grace, abolished the obnoxious tax. Professor Janjiul in his articles on the English Factory Law urged the adoption of a measure for regulating the labour of women and children in Russian factories. The Government followed his advice, and appointed him factory inspector for the district of Moscow.

In short, there is no question of importance relating either to the land, to commerce, or to taxation, which has not been discussed by specialists in our great review. For the contributors to the *Annals* included men who were not alone theoretically acquainted with their subjects, but had seen with their own eyes the workings of the systems which they desired to reform and the evils which they wished to abolish. This lent to it an authority altogether exceptional, and the editor was enabled to enlist in the service of the periodical which he directed the most ardent and intellectual spirits of the time, every one of whom was animated with unbounded zeal to enlighten public opinion and promote the best interests of the country. And yet this great, this priceless publication has been struck down without warning, crushed by the stroke of a Minister's pen, its useful career stopped, and its noble and enthusiastic band of writers silenced and dispersed. Why? In the circular accompanying the decree of suppression the Government gives its reasons for this portentous proceeding. The *Annals*, it is alleged, was a subversive organ, a sort of *Narodnaia Volia* (a clandestine revolutionary print), published in defiance of the censorship. Several of the contributors were affiliated to revolutionary societies, and two members of the editorial staff were politically compromised. The futility of these pretexts is self-evident, especially when it is remembered that out of nearly a hundred contributors not one was punished for these pretended crimes.

We pass now to the accusation in chief, which suggests more important considerations than any of the others. The Ministerial circular charges the

Annals and the Liberal Press generally with having caused all the sad events of recent years (that is to say, the assassinations and other acts of terrorism), with advocating doctrines absolutely identical with those of the clandestine revolutionary organs, with adopting a similar tone, borrowing their methods of exposition, and imitating their literary style.

Readers will remember that only a few years ago the Russian Government proclaimed everywhere that the revolutionary party was recruited solely among the ignorant and the young, from unsuccessful students and men of broken fortunes. Now it openly accuses the entire Liberal Press of having gone over to the enemy with arms and baggage. The importance of the fact, if it is a fact, cannot be overestimated, albeit the prudence of the avowal may well be doubted, for in the Russia of to-day, as in France before the Revolution, all that the country possesses of worth, talent, intelligence, and instruction is found in the ranks of the liberal opposition. The reaction has but incapacities. The only men of talent whom it has secured during the last ten years—from M. Dortoievsky, in *belles lettres*, down to Mr. Katkoff in journalism—are both renegades from the Liberal cause. The former was once a Socialist, and suffered ten years' penal servitude for his connection with the Petrachevsky society; the latter, in his earlier and better years, distinguished himself by his warm advocacy of a constitution on the English model. Even the Souvourins and other minor lights of the reaction were once wanderers in the gardens of liberalism. Yet, as I desire neither to falsify facts nor disguise the truth, even in the seeming interest of the party to which I belong, I am constrained to say that, strongly as the Russian Press is opposed to the Government, it is not a revolutionary force, has not indeed as yet grasped the revolutionary idea.

II.

All who know our literature will agree that its most striking and characteristic tendency is not subversive, or, to speak more plainly, it does not use its influence to bring about a re-organization of our political *régime*. The censor stands effectually in the way of any advocacy in this direction being attempted, and our writers and publicists are too lacking in political instruction to make the attempt. True, they have high instincts and noble aspirations; but the instincts are ill-defined, the aspirations vague and unguided by a clear understanding and a resolute will. They are like a locomotive without rails, their course is erratic, and they are always encountering obstacles and being engulfed in quicksands. The most marked trait in our national literature, that which gives it a character all its own, is its deep-seated democratism, its generous and unselfish sympathy with the poor and lowly. The greater part of our publications are devoted to subjects connected with the well-being of the people and the amelioration of their lot. It is the same with all our leading periodicals. The peasant, his wants and his woes, are always their favourite theme. Nor is this merely a passing fashion. It has been thus for thirty years. If we pass from articles and reviews to *belles lettres*, we are struck by a peculiarity which distinguishes it from the light literature of all other countries. While fiction that deals with the lives of the lowly is elsewhere the exception and occupies an inferior position, in Russia the loves, the sufferings, and the virtues of the peasantry form the favourite and the frequent subjects of our younger and more popular authors. It would be difficult to find a more conclusive proof than this of the prevailing sentiments of our superior classes; for it is they, not the peasants themselves, who read these romances of humble life. This generous democratism of the instructed and well-placed, arises from the conditions and circumstances of our intellectual development; it is the best augury and the surest guarantee for the progress and eventual happiness of the people—once they are the masters of their own fortunes. The sympathy of the instructed classes for the common folk assumes among the leaders of the democratic movement a character peculiar to itself and essentially Russian, and is described by an untranslatable Russian word. The members of this party are called *narodnik*, or, to coin an English equivalent, " peasantists." The origin of this phase of opinion is sufficiently remarkable to merit a few words of explanation. How far it may be due to the deep sense of shame and disgust with which the institution of slavery inspired no inconsiderable portion of our nobility, and the desire thence arising to make some amends to the victims of a bad and degrading system ; how far to the somewhat effusive enthusiasm of the Russian character and its proneness to raise every strong conviction to the dignity of a religious dogma, how far to our unfortunate historic past, which renders it easy for us to sacrifice our individuality on the altar of a cause which we deem high and noble, I will not attempt to determine.

These and several other factors have combined to produce the result in question, for ever since its inception Russian democratism has been marked by characteristics peculiar to itself. The old advocate, Spassovitch, in his speech during the Netchiaeff trial, related that even in his earlier days it was not unusual for young aristocrats to dress as peasants and live among the people. In 1856, some young nobles of certain provinces, notably Tver, Kieff, and others, abandoned the privileges of their rank and inscribed their names in the registers of the rural communes as simple peasants, albeit they were thereby rendered liable to be flogged by a mere order of the police and exposed to other unpleasant possibilities. But the movement alarmed the Government, and was stopped by an ukase in the time of the Minister Lanskoy. It is now no more possible for a Russian noble to become a peasant than for a British peer to become a member of the House of Commons. The democratic party as a whole, although they did not go the length of offering to be flagellated out of love for the people, made enormous sacrifices in the people's cause; not alone material sacrifices, to which none could object, but sacrifices of principle. The instructed classes, nourished on the masterpieces of European literature, could hardly breathe in the stifling atmosphere of Muscovite despotism. They thirsted for political freedom as travellers in an African desert thirst for a drop of cold water. An Englishman in such circumstances would have said, "I need, therefore I will try to have." Said the Russian *narodnik*, "I need, therefore will I resign myself not to have." And if asked for an explanation, he would have added that it was he and his like alone who had need of political freedom; the peasant—chief object of his solicitude—it would profit nothing. Flagrant error, for as touching natural rights there can be no conflict of interests. But this the democrats of 1860 failed to understand, and they agreed to prostrate themselves before the autocracy on the sole condition that it should promise to promote the well-being of the masses. Revolutionists of the stamp of Herzen were unable to resist this tendency, and democrats like Nicolas Milutin (brother of the Minister) and Mouravieff (of the Amour) became humble servants of the Tzar. Than this it was impossible for men to push further the principle of abnegation, or more completely to efface their individuality. Their love was, indeed, like that of the fabled pelican, who fed her little ones with her own flesh. The stupid bird did not see that her death or disablement would of a surety entail the destruction of her offspring. By voluntarily effacing itself the democratic party delivered the people, bound hand and foot, to the venal and cruel bureaucracy which is the true Russian despotism. It was this fatal error that wrecked the great Liberal movement of 1860, although it had the support of the Polish insurrection. The Government found no difficulty in forgetting its promises and preserving intact its prerogatives. When the reaction set in every concession which had been granted was little by little withdrawn because, owing to the policy of the democratic party, no force existed whereby the bureaucracy could be withstood. Hence when, twenty years later, a new Liberal movement was initiated, everything had to be begun afresh. The movement this time, born of the International and the Paris Commune, was purely socialistic. The leaders had no illusions about the autocracy. But as extreme Socialists they are equally opposed to constitutionalism and to monarchy. Their ideal is the supremacy of the working classes. They would pass at one bound from barbarism and despotism to pure Socialism. Here we have a new doctrine, revolutionary peasantism. The idealization of the people has reached its apogee. The people are omnipotent. True, they are ignorant and illiterate, but instead of culture they have a multitude of noble instincts, which will do quite as well. The favourite idea is to provoke an immediate social revolution; the idea of political revolution, of re-organizing the State on a Liberal and constitutional basis is clearly as little favoured by the revolutionary *narodnik* as it was a generation ago by the monarchic *narodnik*. But as no step whatever in advance is possible without political liberty, it is evident that the *narodnik* of both categories are in contradiction with themselves, and their policy can result only in the maintenance of the existing *régime* just as it is, that is to say, of the reaction which now rules Russia with absolute sway. It is the union of these two influences, of the old *narodnik* and the new, that has given birth to the so-called *narodnicestvo*, or literary "peasantism," from which most of our extreme opposition organs draw their inspiration. In these circumstances, as may well be supposed, the political programme of the Democratic Press — not even excepting the *Annals*, which was also *narodnik*—is vague, inconsistent, and unreal. This being the case, and seeing, moreover, that there are journals such as the *Nedeilia*, which, while calling themselves Radical, adopt all the ideas of Souvourin (although they do not thereby avoid prosecution), and others that panegyrize the domestic policy of Prince Bismarck, it cannot seriously be contended that the democratic section of the Russian Press deserves to be called subversive. But there is another section of the same party, also represented in the Press, which claims to be "Liberal" *par excellence*. It professes to be neither *narodnik* nor Slavophile, and advocates, so far as its civic courage permits, the pure principles of European Liberalism. But in renouncing the errors of the older parties these liberals have, at the same time, renounced the principle from which the former cause derives its strength — political Radicalism. Having made moderatism the basis of their political faith, refusing to admit even in theory the idea of any effective protest against tyranny, our so-called Liberals have doomed themselves to complete sterility. For in a country like Russia, where law violates justice, and justice disregards law, moderatism has no place. All that these Liberals can do is to implore the Government to be good enough to resign, and their shameful servility to the powers that be has alienated from them the best of our Russian youth, and all the most potent progressive forces of the nation. Few papers indeed have known how to reconcile in their programme true Liberalism with Radical Democratism—the only programme which has a future in our country. True, they did not advocate these ideas openly—the " censor " would not have allowed it—but it did so " between the lines," and never printed anything incompatible with its principles—which is all we have a right to expect from any Russian journal. Of these papers I will cite only one, the *Slovo* already mentioned. As it is irrevocably suppressed, I may speak well of it, without exposing it to unpleasant consequences.

We may thus safely affirm that our Press has done little for the political enlightenment of Russian society.

The clandestine Press, both abroad and at home, have done far more, notwithstanding lack of means and the difficulty of distribution.

III.

Yet we must give credit where credit is due, and there can be no question that the so-called Liberal and Radical Press, the *Annals* above all, have greatly helped in the development of revolutionary ideas, but in another fashion than by direct teaching. They have laid bare the evils of our social system and political order, proving their charges with undeniable testimony and irrefutable logic. For this sort of propaganda, none the less effective because indirect, it suffices to have a love for truth and to see things as they are; because in the Russia of to-day only the blindest optimism or deliberate bad faith can defend the existing order, and impute, as do the Souvourins and Katkoffs, treason and wickedness to all who venture to cast a doubt on the wisdom or patriotism of the bureaucracy. This explains why the Press, almost without exception, is hostile to the Government. It is impossible in the nature of things that they should be otherwise. No censorship can effectually combat an opposition of this character. The only way to overcome the hostility of the Press is by suppressing all its existing organs and forbidding the establishment of new papers. A Government Press is all but impossible, for, to the honour of Russian journalism be it said, there are to be found in the country few, if any, journalists of the stamp of Mr. Zitovitch, and even if such editors were forthcoming readers would still be lacking.

In the year 1884, therefore, matters stood thus. Of old-established reviews with some influence and a wide circle of readers there remained only one, the *European Messenger*. All the others had been hurried out of existence by the censorship. Among the St. Petersburg reviews there was one, the *Dielo*, which, by an exceptional piece of spitefulness on the part of the Government, had always been censured before publication, thereby causing its conductors numberless embarrassments and continual annoyance. On occasions when the censors were more than usually censorious Mr. Blagosvetloff, the publisher, would be compelled to print five or six times as many sheets as were actually required—150 or 180 instead of thirty. As many as five articles out of six were often rejected by the censorship. (The articles were presented in proof, not in manuscript.) The enormous useless expense incurred in this way may be imagined; but as some set-off to all the proprietors had at least a right to assume that the review would be guaranteed against complete suppression by the Government—if for no other reason because such a proceeding would be a palpable admission of the uselessness of censorship. And in effect the *Dielo* was not suppressed, technically. But all the same a very decided stop was put to its career. The Minister sent for Mr. Ostrogorsky, the nominal editor (who was also a tutor), and told him that he must choose between giving up that position and dismissal from the tutorship by which he made his living. The Minister evidently intended to play the *Dielo* the same trick he had played the *Slovo*. If Mr. Ostrogorsky yielded to the threat and gave up the editorship he would refuse to confirm the appointment of another editor in his place. But Mr. Ostrogorsky preferred to forfeit his means of livelihood rather than abandon the nominal editorship of the review. On this the Minister ordered the acting editor, M. Stanukovitch (M. Blagovetloff's successor) to sell the review to Mr. Wolfson, a man whose opinions were altogether different from those advocated by the *Dielo*, threatening that, in the event of his refusal, the censorship should reject every article presented for approval. In this way the *Dielo* was worse than suppressed; it was transformed into an organ of the reaction.

As I have just observed, one of the old influential Liberal reviews still survives in precarious solitude, the *Messenger* of Mr. Stassulevitch. People have been in daily expectation of its suppression. But as its editor (who has been tutor to several imperial grand dukes), and many of his contributors have friends at court, Count Tolstoi has so far let it alone. How long he will hold his hand it is hard to say. In the meanwhile, however, he was preparing another stroke against his pet detestation—literature and thought. This time he surpassed himself, and his *Index librorum prohibitorum*—list of books excluded from libraries and reading-rooms—caused throughout Russia an astonishment mingled with laughter, which left no room for indignation.

CHAPTER XXXII.

A SAMPLE FROM THE BULK.

In December, 1884, at the Moscow assizes took place the trial of Rykov, once manager of the defunct bank of Skopine, who, by the enormity of his depredations, unmatched even in Russia, has obtained an almost European notoriety. For an entire fortnight the Russian Press—albeit the Moscow papers had received more than one official caution—were simply full of the case. In society hardly any other subject was discussed. It was the burning question of the hour, and will not soon be forgotten. That malversations are often committed by functionaries charged with the care or administration of public funds is in Russia a matter of common knowledge. The public are so used to scandals of this sort that, as a rule, they attract little or no attention. They are regarded as being in the nature of things. To rouse people from their apathy the thieving must present some striking or dramatic feature, or the sums stolen be of startling amount. These features the Rykov case presented in abundance. The malversations of the ex-manager and his confederates are reckoned at 12,000,000 roubles—probably the biggest robbery of the sort ever perpetrated, even in the empire of the Tzar. This alone would have been enough to excite public attention. But when, after two years of waiting and suspense, the shameful secrets of this band of brigands were revealed in open court, the figures, portentous as they were, paled into insignificance as compared with the social and political questions raised by this extraordinary trial. It is from this point of view that the Rykov case merits the attention of English readers. As a drop of water from a well defiled shows all its impurities, so from this trial may be inferred the unspeakable corruption with which, under the present *régime*, the official world of Russia is infected from top to bottom.

The Bank of Skopine was founded in 1863, at a time of considerable industrial activity, and was expected to prove eminently useful to the trade of the district. It was a communal, not a Government institution. On the other hand, the State had very much to do with the bank, for, like all other communal banks, it was placed under the control of the Ministries of the Interior and Finance, and had to render to the latter department a periodical and detailed account of its operations and its position. Rykov was appointed to the managership, although, as everybody knew, he had been guilty, while occupying a previous appointment, of malversation. But the offence was readily overlooked, perhaps for a reason suggested by the Russian proverb, "Only he who has not sinned against God has not robbed the Tzar." True, a few protests were made by the Skopine people. Yet Rykov was sustained by his superiors, and for a short time he seems to have justified their good opinion. But in 1868, as afterwards appeared, there was a deficit of 54,000 roubles. But, being reluctant to publish this unpleasant fact to the world or impart it to the Minister of Finance, he did what, as his advocate ingenuously put it, anybody in his place would have done—drew up a false balance-sheet, and of so satisfactory a character that it attracted deposits from all parts of the country. From this date the affairs of the bank went from bad to worse; but the more desperate became its condition the more brilliant grew its balance-sheets. Though he was doing no legitimate banking business whatever, Rykov, by the offer of $7\frac{1}{2}$ per cent interest on deposits (while other banks were paying five), procured funds in abundance. To show how his exceptional profits were earned, Rykov entered in the bank's books divers ingeniously contrived financial operations. There were fictitious discounts, fictitious loans, fictitious purchases, and fictitious sales. An old man in the pay of the bank, so illiterate that he could hardly write his own name, signed every December a contract for the purchase of several millions worth of imaginary securities, and this transaction, and the resulting imaginary profit thereon, always figured on the bogus balance-sheet presented to the Minister and published in the *Gazette*.

Rykov not alone paid his depositors a high rate of interest, he gave away large sums to charitable institutions, supported schools, and subsidized churches, thereby securing the goodwill of the clergy and acquiring a high reputation for piety and philanthropy, good works and right views. All these gifts, as well as Rykov's own personal expenditure, which was on a lavish scale, were taken from the bank's coffers and entered as payments to dummy customers. The remainder and greater part of the receipts and deposits were simply stolen, either for the manager's own purposes or to buy the silence of his confederates. Paper was made on an extensive scale, and with little attempt at disguise. Antieff, a man of straw, drew on Safoneff, equally a man of straw, for fifty or a hundred thousand roubles, discounted the bill, and got the money. Then the operation would be reversed, and Safoneff get the money. Purely fictitious bills with imaginary names were discounted, and the porters and messengers of the bank figure in the books as debtors for tens of thousands of roubles taken by their master. "Everything was done *en famille*," said one of the witnesses.

But to profit by all this profusion it was necessary to belong to the *clique*, to be either a protector, a kinsman, or an accomplice. Lists of suppliants (*sic*) were laid regularly before Rykov, who, according to his caprice, wrote opposite each name "granted" or "refused." When a bill fell due the acceptor was courteously requested to accept another, including the discount, which, it is hardly necessary to say, nobody ever thought of paying in coin. But after a while even these formalities were dispensed with. When the favoured few wanted money they simply asked for it—sometimes took it without asking. "They took money from the cash box without counting it," said one witness. "They came with a pocket-handkerchief, filled it with banknotes, and went home," testified another.

Such was the method of doing business in the famous bank of Skopine. And the swindle went on, not for a few weeks or months merely, but for something like fifteen long years, an astounding fact even for Russia, and elsewhere unimaginable. In a small provincial town, where everybody knows everybody else, Rykov's doings and the bank's position could not possibly be secret—were, in fact, so widely known that when the crash came, the entire province (Riasan) produced but nineteen unfortunates who had intrusted their savings to Mr. Rykov and his fellow robbers, and among the 6000 customers of the bank not one dwelt in Skopine. How, then, was it possible for irregularities which were known throughout a whole province to escape for fifteen years the attention of the authorities, local and general? How, above all, did they escape the attention of the corporation, for the law places communal banks under the immediate supervision of mayors and municipalities. It is their duty each month to examine the books, count the cash, and overhaul the securities. How was it, then, that all this time, the municipality failed to remark the gross and palpable frauds perpetrated by their manager? The answer is simple. They were privy to the frauds and participators in the plunder. All robbed the bank. Mayor Ikonnikov robbed, Mayor Ovtschinnikov robbed, the Town Clerk robbed, every member of the municipality robbed. The monthly audit was a farce. The books were never looked at, the cash was never counted, the balance-sheet was signed without being examined.

And the authorities, the administration, the police,

usually so vigilant, and, when it is a question of maintaining order or punishing political malcontents, so prompt to act, what were they doing? How could they be blind to facts known to all the world? The same explanation applies to them. They were in the ring; tarred with the same brush as the municipality, and they robbed with the rest. The *ispravnik*, chief of police, was in Rykov's pay. Aleksandroff, the local justice of the peace, called in derision Rykov's lackey, received from the bank a loan of 100,000 roubles and a stipend of 500 roubles a year. His successor, Likareff, was put on a similar footing. The connivance of the smaller official fry, such as the postmaster, the *pristavs* (inferior police), was secured in like fashion, as also the members of the force who acted as the manager's spies. Having thus bought the entire local administration, Rykov became as much the autocrat of Skopine as the Tzar is of All the Russias. He could do whatever he liked, and conducted himself with all the insolence of an ignorant *parvenu*. There dwelt in the town a doctor of the name of Bitni, a man of good repute and highly esteemed for his integrity; but being so unfortunate as to offend Rykov, he was one day ordered by the police to betake himself to the town of Kassimvo and there abide. No reason for this arbitrary proceeding was assigned, and it was only when the day of reckoning came that Dr. Bitni learnt that his expulsion was due to Rykov, who had remarked to the *ispravnik* that the doctor was an "evil-intentioned man." On this hint the chief of police had acted. A young fellow named Sokoloff was so ill-advised as to whistle while passing the manager in the public garden of Skopine. Rykov chose to look on this as an insult, and, the *ispravnik* taking the same view of the matter, the youth was exiled by administrative order. With Mr. Orloff, an engineer, it fared even worse. He was sent by a company to purchase some coal, the produce of a mine owned by the bank in the province of Riasan. But finding the article of indifferent quality, he refused, on behalf of his employers, to accept it, and, being presumably an honest man, he was not to be corrupted by the bribes which were no doubt offered to him. Be that as it may, Rykov charged Mr. Orloff with incendiarism, had him arrested, and sentenced to a term of imprisonment, from which he was only saved by the intervention of the Imperial Procurator-General from undergoing. "The police of Skopine," said the witness Lanskoy, whose evidence was quoted in the indictment, "was ready at any moment to execute Rykov's least desire." The (two) brothers, Lanskoy, Sokoloff, and Tinogenoff, all *employés* of the bank, lodged in the house of a Mr. Brigneff, an arrangement which, for some inexplicable reason, did not suit Rykov's purpose. So without more ado he ordered the police to remove them, and the order was duly carried into effect. They were one day waited on by the *ispravnik*, Kobelinzky, and three policemen, and compelled to leave their lodgings forthwith. Nor was this all. Rykov counted so confidently on the support of the local representatives of the Government that he lorded it over everybody, openly rated the fire brigade because they did not conduct themselves to his satisfaction at a fire, and, vexed by some show of independence on the part of the chief of police, told him that he had better take care what he was about. "You are nobody very particular," said Rykov, "and I have only to say a word to have sent down on your place a whole waggon-load of *ispravniks*." When, in order to ruin Mr. Diakonov, who, unfortunately for himself, owed the bank 10,000 roubles, he had this gentleman's house seized and offered for sale by auction, not a single bidder appeared on the scene, so great was the fear inspired by the all-powerful manager. This was exactly what Rykov desired. The house was worth 30,000 roubles; he made the complaisant police value it at 9000, and had the unfortunate Mr. Diakonov cast into prison, where he remained for eleven months. In this way an almost illiterate man—for the manager could only just read and write—became absolute master of Skopine. "God alone could contend against Rykov," said one of the witnesses.

But, it may be asked, were there not among this mass of cowardice, servility, and corruption a few just men, with sufficient public spirit to bring the doings of the Nabob of Skopine to the notice of the higher authorities, who could not possibly have yielded to his influence or accepted his bribes? Yes, certainly, there were several. One of them was the ill-fated Diakonov, and he had his reward. And then there was the ex-mayor, Leonoff, who gave evidence on the trial. While he was in office the affairs of the bank were kept in order, the books properly audited, the cash and securities regularly overhauled. But this did not suit Rykov's purpose; he bribed the electors and the municipality; Leonoff was turned out of office and a more complaisant mayor chosen in his place. Yet, though no longer a magistrate he did not cease his endeavours to protect the bank from the depredations of its managers. So far back as 1868 Leonoff and several other citizens addressed a petition to General Boldireff, governor of the province, in which they set forth the condition of the bank, and prayed him to order an inquiry. In 1874—six years afterwards—came the answer. It was to the effect that, the petition not being drawn up according to the prescribed form, no action could be taken thereupon. In 1878 another like attempt was made, the authority appealed to in this instance being the Minister of the Interior. The answer was as characteristic as before. As the document did not carry the proper stamp (20 kopecks, 5d.), the prayer of the petitioners could not be taken into consideration. On this the petitioners drew up another address correctly stamped, and sent that to the Minister, expecting that this time, at least, something would be done. "But," said one of them (Maslennikoff), when giving his evidence, "we have not received an answer to this day."

This indifference in high quarters is as easily explained as the voluntary blindness of the local administration. Boldireff, the governor of the province, was bribed like the rest. He received from Rykov 79,000 roubles. Volkov, the vice-governor, did better; he got 100,000 roubles. The Marshal of the Nobility sold himself for a paltry 12,000 roubles. When the inquiry was ordered in 1882 this gentleman found it convenient to be abroad. The Councillor of the Provincial Government, Koumiantzev, the members of the Tribune, Babine and Kirmilitzin, and the Procurator Pottavzki, were proved to have been all in the same boat.

The trial failed to furnish proofs equally convincing as to the parts played by the bureaucracy of

St. Petersburg. Nobody cared to sift this side of the question—neither the President of the Court, the Crown Prosecutor, nor the prisoner's advocate. No functionary in the Ministry of the Interior was either summoned as a witness or required to explain his conduct. But Rykov hinted darkly that certain highly placed personages deserved much more than he to stand in the prisoners' dock. The hints of a man like Rykov are very far from being trustworthy evidence, but several facts came to light which confirm in a measure the suspicions they suggest. For instance, a mysterious personage named Bernard, a civil general, acted as the manager's diplomatic agent at St. Petersburg, and arranged delicate matters for him in high quarters. As recompense for his services he received a million roubles—nominally as a loan. In the end they had a quarrel, and Bernard contrived to rid himself of his liability by an expedient as simple as it was significant. He applied to his particular friend, General Tcherevin, chief of of the gendarmery, who thereupon requested the manager of the bank at Skopine to return General Bernard his acceptances, amounting to 500,000 roubles. Rykov did as he was asked. It was hardly conceivable, however, that the chief's eloquence could alone have persuaded the manager to so great generosity. What, then, was the consideration that

Rykov received, and the service which the other, a great man in the Third Section, rendered? This mystery the trial left unsolved, but the names of some other personages of high position figured in the proceedings—not greatly to their advantage. The Emperor's Adjutant-General, Grabbe, owed the bank 242,000 roubles; Prince Obolinski owed it 60,000, and both debts were set down as "bad." How came it that these gentlemen, neither of whom were connected either with commerce or finance, were able to obtain from the bank these large sums? When Rykov was pressed on the point, all he had to say was that he had lent them the money "under the guarantee of their high titles." But the explanation may be hazarded that he found it necessary to spend money at St. Petersburg promiscuously and without stint. In Russia you cannot move a step without paying. Rykov was well received everywhere and made much of by great people. On the days of grand solemnity Ministers sent him congratulatory despatches. "How much did these despatches cost them?" exclaimed the other day a Russian paper with seeming simplicity. And how much, we may ask, cost him the decorations and titles which were so lavishly conferred upon him? A striking proof of the tenderness with which, even to the last, the arch-rogue and his accomplices were treated by the authorities was mentioned by the *Russian Courier* of December 31, 1882. "Although," it wrote, "the Commission (of Inquiry) is working with zeal, the seizure of the property of Rykov's confederates proceeds very slowly. The accused, to the manifest detriment of the bank's creditors, have every opportunity of concealing and disposing of their assets. Ikonnikov (the mayor), notwithstanding the charges against him and his approaching trial, sends every night loads of merchandise out of the town. The seizure of the property of the other thirteen confederates did not take place until a month after their committal to trial."

The exposure of the frauds and the punishment of the criminals was due to the efforts of the three or or four honest citizens already mentioned, Leonoff, Popoff, and Rausoff, and the courage of a single newspaper. If these men had not been ex-members of the municipality and well-to-do they would have learnt to their cost what it was to denounce a Councillor of Commerce and chevalier of several orders. Utterly unable to make any impression on the local administration, or to obtain a hearing from the higher authorities, they did that which in Russia is looked upon as a doubtful and desperate expedient, but which in any other country would have been done at the outset—they appealed to the Press. But even here the irrepressible manager barred the way. For two years the letters they despatched to various papers never reached their destination ; they were stopped at the post-office. According to the evidence of the witness Simonoff, evidence which was not gainsaid, Peroff, the postmaster, received from Rykov 50 roubles per mensem in consideration of which he intercepted and handed to his employer every letter addressed to a newspaper which came into the office, and any others that the manager wanted. Atlaroff, the telegraphist, rendered in his department analogous services on similar terms. It was only in 1882 that the gentlemen in question succeeded in getting printed in the *Russian Courier* several letters on the affairs of the bank of Skopine. The journal which did this good service for the community is one of the few liberal organs left, and it has been harried and persecuted by the Government to the verge of extinction. Other papers, either because they were paid to keep silence or hesitated to attack an institution so closely connected with the State, and enjoying the confidence of so many " supporters of order," refused to publish any letters whatever on the subject. Mr. Katkoff, the celebrated editor of the *Moscow Gazette*, had the questionable honour of being publicly praised by Rykov as one of his greatest and most esteemed benefactors !

The letters in the *Courier* were the death sentence of the Skopine Bank. Creditors rushed from all parts of the country to withdraw their deposits; but the run ceased almost as soon as it began, for the strong room, instead of containing the twelve million roubles shown on the balance-sheet, was empty, and the bill-cases were filled with bogus paper. The bank fell, and great was the fall therof. The scandal and the panic it caused spread far and wide, confidence was at an end, and there was a run on nearly every communal bank in Russia. A few stood the test, but a full dozen came to the ground, and when their affairs were looked into they were found to be pretty much in the same condition as those of the bank of Skopine.

Among others, the bank of Kamychin (province of Saratoff) had to close its doors, and, when inquisition was made, serious irregularities were discovered; the mayor of the town and several of its richest merchants were arrested and put on their trial. They had depleted the bank of the whole of its paid-up capital and its reserve, for which there was nothing to show but worthless paper. It was the bank of Skopine over again, but on a less scale. At Krolevez (province of Tchernigoff) the entire *personnel* of the communal bank were placed under arrest, the charge against them being that, in collusion with several tradesmen of the place, they had committed extensive malversations. The manager and assistant manager of the bank of Roslavl (province of Smolensk), which also broke, were convicted of having embezzled 28,000 roubles of the bank's money. The accounts of this establishment had not been audited for eleven years. At Tamboff the inquisition brought to light quite a multitude of malversations. When the manager wanted to oblige a friend and still keep up a show of regularity, he would discount his draft on his wife and provide for the bill at maturity by reversing the operation. Similar discoveries have been made and prosecutions instituted at Voronez, Kotelnich, Kozloff, and other places, and the papers announce that Airloff, ex-manager of the bank of Orel, and all his colleagues in the direction, are charged with misappropriating 4,000,000 roubles of the bank's money. As their defalcations were spread over twelve years, the case is not unlike that of Skopine.

So much for banks, but it is not bank managers and directors alone who rob their employers and betray their trust. Robbery is the rule, honesty the exception. Robbery goes on in every department of the State. In 1882 a Russian paper, the *Sovremenn Tzvestia* gave a list of the " great robberies " known to have been committed during the last few years by public functionaries. According to this account there were twenty-five thefts of from 20,000 to 60,000 roubles each; six ranging from 400,000 to 500,000; and six ranging from one million to twelve millions—in all, twenty-seven millions. This is exclusive of small affairs of less than 20,000 roubles, which are past counting. "Russia has in its service but two honest men, you and me," said the Emperor Nicolas to his eldest son, and whatever progress the country may have made since his time has certainly not extended to the character of its public servants.

One of the most significant facts brought out by recent revelations is the relatively modest part played by the representatives of the Central Government. In the matter of the banks, the agents of the local and superior administrations acted merely as accomplices and receivers of stolen goods. The active parts and the lion's share were taken by high-placed rogues, who were enabled to rob with impunity by subsidizing the venal army of *tchinovniks*, always ready to place at the disposal of the highest bidder the arbitrary powers with which they are intrusted. It may even be said that the inferior agents of authority have been more in fault than the higher representatives of the State. The latter intervene only in exceptional cases; smaller robberies are left to be dealt with by the local administrations.

During Rykov's trial he protested warmly and

often against what he called the injustice of the public and the Press. "They say that I am a monster; that I have stolen six millions. It is a gross calumny. I swear before you, gentlemen of the jury, that I stole but one million; one million only," he protested with indignant gesture and unconscious humour. This was quite true, as his young advocate triumphantly proved. For his personal use Rykov had taken only a million. But he had been enabled to take that million, only by spending five millions more as hush-money. The Government by which Russia has the misfortune to be ruled is for the country pretty much what Rykov was for the bank. In order to obtain money for its own use it must connive at the depredations of its own agents. To maintain its prerogatives the central despotism must tolerate the despotism of thousands of local autocrats, governors, policemen, and *ispravniks*. To shield itself from criticism, the State must suppress freedom of speech, muzzle the Press, and, for fear lest the latter should expose the abuses of the system, forbid it to expose the malpractices of individuals.

To show fully what the *tchinovniks* of the White Tzar are I should have to rake up the scandalous trial of Boush, of the commissariat, tell the story of the Minister Makoff's suicide, make extracts from the bloodstained pages of the "Revision of Oufa and

Siberia." There are things far more serious than the small pedantry of the Minister of the Interior in refusing to read a petition because it is insufficiently stamped, or the humour of a Minister of Finance in paternally recommending a forger to renounce his dangerous practices. But it is not within my present purpose to describe the Russian bureaucracy. I have exposed the case of the Skopine Bank only to give some idea of another peculiarity of the present Government—the facilities which it offers to the dishonest, who so turn to account the prevailing system as to rob and ruin the country with impunity. It is easy to see from this episode what are the men who are filling the places left vacant by those whom the Government, by its laws and administrative measures, has excluded from all participation in public affairs on the ground of their suspected liberal tendencies. Whilst the most modest attempt to render the country honest service may endanger a man's liberty, thieves and scoundrels can count on the most ample protection. For dishonesty is the surest guarantee of a man's freedom from the taint of disaffection, and that he has approved himself a trustworthy supporter of the existing order.

CHAPTER XXXIII.

RUSSIA AND EUROPE.

I.

Now we must stop. Our journey must end. It has been a very hurried one, and we could see only a small part of what is worth seeing. Thus far we have pointed out the principle and the spirit of the existing *régime;* we have exposed the conduct of the Government toward the superior—the instructed—classes, which, however numerically small, accomplish most important functions social life. It is over this limited field of governmental action that we must now take a retrospective glance.

Strange spectacle! Here are a State and a Government calling themselves national and patriotic, which systematically from year to year do things that the most barbarous conqueror could do only in some sudden access of wild rage and stupid fanaticism.

For, without a shadow of exaggeration, the exploits of our rulers of to-day can be compared with those of the celebrated Kaliph of Egypt alone. Surely in no other country was such a government ever seen. If all we have exposed were not proved, and doubly proved, by heaps of official documents, we might be tempted to disbelieve it. But it is all unhappily only too true; and, what is still worse, will always be true so long as the autocracy rules in Russia.

Some optimist may be disposed to say that the policy of the Russian triumvirate is but a temporary aberration, caused by the overweening influence over the Emperor of Pobedonotzeff, Katkoff, and Tolstoi. Yes, the policy of the present Government is surely an aberration; but only by reason of its lack of policy, and its cynical frankness. If Pobedonotzeff and Katkoff lose their influence, and Tolstoi should fall, his successor may prove less rash and more cautious. As to the main characteristics of domestic policy, it must needs remain unaltered. The most elementary consideration of self-defence will render it imperative to preserve its main features. At the end of the nineteenth century the sole safeguard of the autocracy consists in the ignorance of the people. It is not enough to confiscate books and suppress liberal papers; the only way to get rid of propagandism is to suppress readers. If peasants read nothing but the *Moscow Gazette*, they will find in the columns relating to "foreign affairs," reports of European politics, of parliaments and free meetings, and many other things, which will equally "instigate" to disrespect of the existing Government. If they limit their reading to *Souvorin's Almanac*, they will find in it accounts of the incidence and distribution of taxation which, rightly understood, may prove as inflammatory as a revolutionary appeal. At the same time, the Government is constrained to shut out society from all part in the management of public affairs. On whom can the autocracy rely but on the police and the bureaucracy? And even against the latter, as everybody knows, it must take precautions.

After being driven into flagrant contradiction with culture, and to open war with the whole body of the instructed classes, the autocracy is now forced into conflict with the State itself. It is prompting the very State to ruin by both hands. By opposing instruction in every shape, it dries up the very sources of national labour. By leaving the management of all, or nearly all, public affairs in the hands of an uncontrollable bureaucracy, as incompetent as it is corrupt, the autocracy diminish the original paucity of their resources by the malversations of their servants. The gradual impoverishment of the State, the growing confusion of the finances, the progressive misery of the tillers of the soil, are but the natural and unavoidable consequences of the existing *régime*. And this is just what we are witnessing in Russia.

II.

These anomalies cannot last. In one way or another the catastrophe must come. There are observers who find many points of likeness between modern Russia and France before the Revolution. There is a good deal of analogy, indeed; the greatest being as touching Russia the diffusion throughout all classes of the nation of anti-governmental tendencies, and of those generous and creative ideas which are called " subversive," because they tend to subvert wrong and institute right. Neither are the material condition and moral dispositions of the masses unlike. There is, however, one vast difference on which we must dwell a moment, because it must contribute greatly to quicken and intensify the decomposition of the Russian State, and hasten the ultimate crisis. It lies in the political position of Russia.

The France of the seventeenth century was surrounded by States as despotic as herself. Russia's neighbours are constitutional States. Their constitutions are very far from being the ideal of freedom. But in any case they prevent their Governments from being at open war with their peoples. Neither Prussia, nor Austria, nor any other Government in Europe willingly prevents the diffusion of education, or the more economical and reasonable management of public affairs, out of fear of strengthening their enemies. All neighbouring States are growing in strength and riches. All Governments do their best to promote general progress, which turns to their advantage. In Russia progress is either non-existent or extremely slow, being checked on every hand by the Government.

Now, being indissolubly united with other European States by political ties—being obliged to sustain an economical, military, and political competition with neighbouring States, Russia is evidently drawing nearer to ruin. For she cannot, without overstraining, keep pace with them, notwithstanding the growing difference in the interior development of the respective countries. The longer this competition lasts, the more disastrous it becomes, the more difficult for Russia to sustain. The political crisis is, therefore, much nearer, more forcible, and imminent than the social crisis. And the actual position of Russia in this regard presents a great analogy with the position of Russia herself in the period which preceded the reforms of Peter the Great. The autocracy plays now just the same part as touching culture as the Moscovite clericalism played in the sixteenth and seventeenth centuries. After being instrumental in the creation of Russian political power, it is now the cause of its gradual destruction. If the autocracy does not fall under the combined effects of interior causes, the first serious war will overthrow it, shedding perhaps rivers of blood and dismembering the State. The destruction of the autocracy has become a political as well as social and intellectual necessity. It is required as well for the safety of the State as for the welfare of the nation.

III.

Let us pass to the central power itself. It is very edifying, and surely most consoling, to see how certain crimes against humanity are in themselves the punishment of the criminals. The Bible records the legend of a Babylonian Tzar of old—Nebuchadnezzar—who, in punishment of his excessive pride, was transformed by the Almighty into an ox, and for twelve years ate nothing but grass. I do not remember why the pride of Babylonian Tzar should have incurred so dire a punishment. Surely it was not greater than the pride of his *confrère* of St. Petersburg, who pretends to govern all, to decide for all, arbitrate for all, and say what is doing and to be done in a nation of a hundred millions. It is quite just that the punishment inflicted on him should be something very (if not altogether) similar, and that he should be condemned to masticate all his life long nothing but paper.

In a bureaucratic State, where everything is done in writing, and nothing left to personal freedom and initiative, the most trifling matters ascend from the inferior agents of the system up to the topmost —the Tzar. What, for instance, will the reader think of the following, one out of thousands of quite similar, "all highest orders," as they are called in official language—the Tzar's ukases. It refers to nothing more nor less than to students' blouses. I transcribe it in all its bureaucratic candour :—

"Having heard the all-humblest report (so the document ran) of the Minister of the State Domain, his Majesty the Emperor—15th October of the current year (1884)—all highly deigned to order, in supplement to the model dresses all-highly approved by his Majesty, the 3rd May, 1882, to the students of the Moscow Agricultural Academy, is granted permission during the lessons in the academy, and in practical work, to wear blouses; the winter, of brown-grey woollen stuff, the summer, of light yellow (unbleached) linen, with a brown leather strap adorned with a metallic clasp, on which, interwoven with a crown of spikes, must be drawn the letters P. and A. in Old Slav character."

Can the time of the supreme ruler of one hundred

millions be better employed than with deep questions as to the colour and material of students' blouses, whether they wear blouses or jackets, or the letters on the clasps are in Slav or Gothic character? This question is not very complicated, it is true. If the Tzar have no particular taste for tailoring, he may settle it at once. But this draft order must be read over to him before being signed; must at least be mentioned to him. He must give his yes or no; must lose a part of his time. And if every Minister bring him a hundred such trifles, how much of his working-time will the Tzar keep for things that are not trifles? And it is easy to see that any Minister can produce as many trivialities as are required to fill up his master's leisure, and deprive him of all possibility of giving serious attention to matters of importance. Thus the Tzar can only act by his Minister's advice. Even such a zealous absolutist as the defunct Moscow Professor Buslaeff, in a letter published in one of our antiquarian magazines, after computing the enormous quantity of useless ukase signing, exclaims that to restore to the White Tzar his liberty of action a part of this futile, everyday, governmental drudgery must be put on a responsible Minister. Yet the learned professor would not go as far as to make him responsible before a national representation. If we compare the position of the despots of various epochs, we may fairly affirm that the present mode of reducing to impotence the would-be all-powerful master is much more effective than the old one. A despot like the old Russian Tzars with an effort of will might have freed himself, though remorsefully from one or another futility of court observance. The chief of modern bureaucratic despots may not, with the same calmness of mind, shun the duty of reading a dozen voluminous suits on the decision of which are pending as many destinies, or a project of financial reform on which may depend the welfare or misery of a province.

And if it should happen that, notwithstanding material obstacles, the Tzar under some particular influence desired to enforce his own view on a subject, the would-be all-humblest executioners thereof, the Ministers, would have no difficulty in arranging the matter. They have only to utilize the marvellous slowness of bureaucratic proceedings, which permits the postponement of every measure for as many years —I could say as many generations—as may be required. Nothing prevents Ministers from effecting at the first opportunity whatever change in the Tzar's decision they like. If they do not they can leave the matter to sleep in some office the sleep of the just. The history of our administration is but a long series of similar instances. If Alexander II. did something in the beginning of his reign, it was only because he broke for a short time with bureaucratic routine, and appealed to society. From the moment when, prompted by fear, he threw himself into the arms of bureaucracy, he became powerless, and went straight to his ruin. Of all sorts of despots that history knows, the most helpless are surely the bureaucratic despots of our time.

We may go still further. As a rough rock of the mountain by long rolling in the bottom of a stream is reduced to a smooth, inoffensive pebble, heavy perhaps, but not sharp, so is the actual autocracy of Russia. The Tzars of old had for their political insignificance a consolation and compensation in unlimited power of self-indulging mischief, if it may be called a consolation. This latter power in our modern Tzars is reduced to quite a platonic kind. There is the all-seeing, all-knowing reporter, with his shrieks and his laughter, his indignation and scandal, to limit their despotism in the inner circle where they move. Our forefathers said, that to be near the Tzar was to be near to death. But a modern Tzar no longer condemns to death by a contraction of his brows as did the Moscow Tzar. Neither does he exile to Siberia the courtiers who incur his displeasure, like the first emperors of the St. Petersburg period. All is done now by *tchinovniks*. Personally, a modern Tzar harms nobody, and is just as quiet and inoffensive as any constitutional monarch. He has not given up his power; he is like a beast with strong teeth and murderous claws which he never uses. He is quite a tame, domesticated animal, who wears obediently the yoke of the courts. With self-denial worthy of a better cause, he is serving as a screen to their misdeeds, exposing himself to all the just consequences of his assumed all-powerfulness which makes his life miserable, his existence a continual fear, his power a derision, his position a disgrace.

The evolution of autocracy is indeed complete. For it could hardly descend lower, it could hardly present a more exhilarating, pleasant, exalting spectacle to its enemies.

IV.

But how? Is it possible that a man without being a fool can act in so strange a fashion? How can he remain in so disagreeable a position, causing thereby the misery of a whole nation, who, after all, have done him no wrong? How can he refuse to redress public wrongs and better his own life by a stroke of the pen—if it were possible? If he does not, it is evident that in reality he cannot. There must be some hidden force and hidden party which holds a power over him. Such a supposition is very common, and it has given rise at various times to theories about the existence of some extremely powerful court party, to which sometimes the name of "old aristocratic," at others that of "old Slavophile" party is given, and so forth. They alone, it is said, prevent the Tzar from doing that good to his country which personally he would be quite disposed to do.

It is strange how extremes sometimes meet. Just the same idea—just in the same shape—rises in the minds of Russian peasants, and is answered nearly in the same way. Only with the peasant imagination gives these hypotheses quite a fantastical dress. Sometimes the legend assumes the character of a dramatic performance, where the good principle embodied in the Tzar is overpowered by the opposite force embodied now in the Senate (usually confounded with the Synod, a permanent ecclesiastic council), now in the Minister (always in a single person, for the peasant thinks there is only one Minister, as there is only one Tzar). Occasionally these legends give the part of bad genius to some member of the imperial family. During the reign of Alexander II. this not too flattering part was usually conferred on the Tzarevitch (the present Tzar); who fills his place now that he has become Tzar himself, I do not know. Somebody does, we may be quite sure. Many pages might be filled with accounts of the *naïve* and childish contrivances by which the peasants try to preserve what remains of their belief in the Tzar against the rude assaults of everyday wrongs inflicted by his orders.

But only the peasantry indulge in such reveries. And even they will abandon them so soon as some glimpse of culture reaches their minds. Instructed Russia has given them up long ago, knowing perfectly that nothing of the kind exists in Russia. The tales about old Slavophile and old aristocratic parties, and such like, have quite the same value as the peasants' legends about the rascality of the Synod or the cunning of the Senate. Never in the course of our history were the upper classes able to acquire any political strength of their own. The reader remembers how our *soi-disant* aristocracy was created, and what it was of old. Such it has remained for all time. In the first century after the transfer of the capital to St. Petersburg it seemed to be otherwise. Situated in a far remote, freshly conquered country, St. Petersburg was but a vast military camp. Its lower classes were composed of foreign Finnish tribes; its upper classes of military and civil officers, most of whom were of foreign origin. Pretorian insurrections were extremely easy in such a town, and ambitious foreigners and courtiers were able sometimes to put their foot on their master's neck. This was due not to the strength of the aristocracy, but to the momentary dislocation of the State. These times, however, have long ago passed away. If there should be a court revolution, it will be directed against the autocracy as a principle, and reckoned on the immediate support of the progressive elements of the whole country. A violent change of government without a change of principles is an utter impossibility. A *coup d'état,* in order to raise himself a step in court hierarchy, will hardly now cross the mind of a modern Field-Marshal Minich. At the court there is no force whatever to oppose effectually the will of the Tzar. There is no political body, no aristocracy, no statesmen even, in the European sense of the word. We have only courtiers— a type already forgotten in Europe, because Russia is the only unhappy country where one will makes laws for millions. And what is a courtier? He is a man in whom training, from generation to generation, has developed to the highest degree effectiveness one single capacity — that of enforcing his will on the sovereign, while making him believe he is obeyed. All other capacities, all feelings, all inclinations, as things useless and even hurtful,

are repressed and gradually destroyed in these ignoble specimens of the human race called courtiers. Now the thing which is the most dangerous and disagreeable impediment to the courtier's efforts is undoubtedly what is called political convictions—strong political opinions. Such things are not to be found in a despotic court. A courtier may accept a political banner as he accepts a dress in a courtly parade, when these afford better chances to currying favour with his master. I will not multiply proofs of things so evident. As a matter of curiosity rather than illustration, let us consider for a moment Mr. Tolstoi. There is no man whose reactionary convictions seem to be more irreconcilable, more deeply rooted. And yet this very pillar of reaction in 1859, only a few years before his appearance as Minister of the white terror and obscurantism, published at Brussels a very interesting pamphlet bearing the title " Voice from Germany."*
Treating of the European politics of the epoch, the author exposes his views and political convictions in general. He is all for liberalism, for constitutional guarantees, for respect to the will of the nation. He pities the Hanoverian Government, which

---

* " Une Voix d'Allemagne," par le Comte Dmitry Tolstoy. Bruxelles : Muguardt, editeur, 1859.

has on its side only the officers of the Government, whilst all the country is against it (p. 7)—just the case in Russia now. Still less satisfied is the liberal count with the conduct of the Government of Bavaria where the king maintained in power, for full nine years, a Minister quite odious to the country (pp. 6, 7)—just the case of Mr. Tolstoi in Russia. He expresses the hope that the rulers of the various German states "will not follow the pernicious example of Hanover, and crush by police reprisals the lawful aspirations of their subjects" (p. 61). "Because," he says, "to put obstacles in the way of the progressive reforms, when they become urgent, is as dangerous as to appeal to insurrection : it is setting fire to the edifice from another corner" (p. 61). He is a strong adversary of clericalism, and stigmatizes "this monstrous alliance of liberalism with popery" (p. 12). He is very severe on Napoleon III., in whom he cannot put confidence, because "he fights for the freedom of foreigners whilst suppressing freedom at home" (p. 14). And he is full of noble indignation against despotic governments, which "having little sympathy with the aspiration of their countries, shout, 'Let us have war!' wanting war in order that people may forget what they are, and let them live at this price" (p. 10)—just what he is urging the Tzar to do now.

All this is taken from a copy of the *brochure* I had

the good luck to procure myself. All this Count Dmitry Tolstoi, the present Minister, wrote with his own hand in the year 1859. He had hardly the time to return from his journey abroad when his liberalism vanished away. In the year 1859 the influence of Grand Duke Constantine (brother of Alexander II.) was in power. It was the epoch of constitutional aspirations. In 1863 Prince Gagarin and the anti-abolitionist party came to the front. Count Dmitry Tolstoi, at a moment's notice, changed the inmost of his soul's convictions and became the right hand of most sordid reaction.

From people of this sort a sovereign has no reason to fear opposition. If the Tzar resolved to change his politics he would have only a sign to make: half of his court would take at once the colour required—from deep red to the most tender blue—provided by this they could secure for themselves the best places.

V.

But as surely as there is no material obstacle which could prevent the Tzar from changing his policy, as surely will no such change ever be initiated by the will of the Tzar.

There are moral and intellectual impossibilities no

less insurmountable than material obstacles. Despots are trained as well as courtiers, even more carefully than courtiers. If the despotism exercised by one transforms the whole court into a school of servility, on the other hand, the crowd of courtiers react on their master whom they surround and educate from his very childhood. One thing generates the other. The courtier is the counterfeit of the despot; the despot is the counterfeit of the courtier. And both mutually demoralize each other. If the courtiers have an insurmountable aversion to free institutions because they will render useless the only accomplishment they possess, the despot clings to this eternal show of flunkeyism and obsequiousness, to this making a man rise and fall by a single word, to all this show of omnipotence however void it may be. If continual effort to study and obey the caprices of one man narrows the minds of courtiers, disabling them to take any comprehensive view, the artificial life of the court and its base desires produce around the despot a sort of intellectual vacuum which renders him still narrower minded than his courtiers.

Having the power to transform into act every thought, every whim, he is preserved from all that may suggest to him such thoughts or whims. It is the fact that there is not a single man in the hundred and one millions of the Tzar's subjects who is more watched or observed in his personal intercourse, whose intellectual food is submitted to stricter censorship, or more carefully selected, than the Tzar's. He reads only extracts of what is thought good for him to know; he does not meet with anybody whom his courtiers would like him to shun. There are hundreds of ways to obtain this effect without seeming to impose on the sovereign's pleasure. And that is done, and has been done, for years and generations; and not only with the Tzar himself, but with every member of his family.

What is more hopeless than the depravity of despotism is the utter, hardly realizable ignorance prevailing in the court on the commonest questions and most elementary conditions of the country they are ruling. We must read the memoirs of Senator Solovieff, and other men connected with the former reign; we must hear the professors of universities who have been allowed to deliver private lectures to small Grand Dukes, and to speak to them occasionally; we must give a glance to the leaders of Mr. Katkoff's *Gazette*, which may be said to be destined for the personal edification of the Emperor and his family—to form some idea of this strange, sophisticated, intellectual world, in which our masters live. There is no absurdity about the condition of Russia that may not be believed there, and the commonest truisms will seem as strange as if they had been told of Saturn. It would not be at all surprising if the Tzar believed Mr. Tolstoi's policy as to the public instruction to be the very embodiment of progress. Did not Mr. Katkoff say it in his leaders, affirming, for instance, that in this point Russia is far more advanced than England. When Count Tolstoi fell into temporary disgrace and was removed from the post of Minister of Public Instruction there was joy in all Russia, as if the country had been freed from a public calamity. Eyewitnesses say that fathers joined in thanksgiving for the blessing of being, on behalf of their children, liberated from the fear of having their career ruined and their hopes destroyed. Yet it would not be at all surprising, however, if the Emperor were to think that he had given great satisfaction to the country in recalling Count Tolstoi to power, and fears that if he were to dismiss him all Russia would be inundated with tears. No absurdity, however gross, would be surprising, and we have many evidences of blunders no less enormous. We must transport ourselves many centuries back, and substitute the effect of time for the effect of social distance to realize something of the intellectual bewilderment of our rulers and masters. A scholar of Averroes' time resuscitated would present in our time no greater confusion in his ideas on science than our rulers on interior politics.

And what shall we say about voluntary misrepresentations, about phantom and imaginary dangers, invented by courtiers in order to impress, to puzzle, and frighten their master, who being on such a greater height is so easily alarmed? The Senator Solovieff's memoir shows that Tzar Alexander II. was seriously afraid of such an absurdity as a murderous attempt from the part of anti-abolitionists! I have been told by a competent person that for some time Count Loris Melikoff was held up to the present Emperor as a threatening bogey of a court revolutionist! It will be not at all surprising if he is replaced now by some military general of the Komaroff or Scobeleff type.

Only a man with exceptional firmness of character, extraordinary courage, and, above all, quite superior intellectual capacity, might contrive to break these invisible intellectual and moral ties, and catch now and then a glimpse of truth. A man who is not favoured by nature, a man who although born in the purple is short of intellectual power, such a man must inevitably yield to the incessant efforts of a crowd of eager, unscrupulous people, who with all their incapacity for real business make leading their master by the nose a science, playing on him as on a fiddle, and putting everything to their profit—his caprices and his aspirations, his good and his bad humours, his foibles and stubbornness, his vices and his virtues, if he has any.* No, the crowned heads of our time cannot take any effective part in the management of State affairs. They are organically incapable of doing it. They cannot govern, let them reign then, as long as people cannot do without them. If they attempt to do more they can but receive the due punishment to themselves which is a curse for the nation: they become marionettes whose wires are pulled by unseen courtiers, as unscrupulous as they are irresponsible. To hope in a Tzar's sudden

---

* The reader will allow me to give a little amusing anecdote of very little significance but quite authentic and characteristic, how the most simple contrivance serves to make a fool of the Tzar. It happened in the first years of Alexander III.'s reign, to a Samara nobleman of the name of K——. He wanted a Govermental allowance of 200,000 roubles to start a leather manufactory. Many large Russian manufacturers get considerable sums of State money "as an encouragement of national industry." All was arranged well. Everybody who had to be bribed was bribed. Mr. K—— was quite sure of success, so far that, returning to Samara, he did not choose to wait the few weeks that remained before the Emperor's definitive confirmation, and borrowed from a Tartar merchant the sum promised him, and set to work at once. Great was his disappointment and despair when he received a telegram stating bluntly that the Emperor did not confirm the allowance. He rushes to St. Petersburg to his protectors. How? What is it? Nobody knew. All was done right, as promised. But the Emperor refused. A whim took him. It is quite incomprehensible. We cannot help it. Mr. K—— deemed himself a ruined man. But one fine morning, when he left the Minister of the Interior he was followed by a *holonatchalink*, head clerk of one of the numerous offices. The man asked him plainly if he consented to give him the sum of 10,000 roubles if the thing was put right. Mr. K—— ex-

change of mind is to hope in the courtier's turning suddenly honest, willing to sacrifice their ambitions and interests to the weal of the country.

No ; it is sheer madness to hope that the political re-organization of Russia can be effected by the initiative of the Tzar himself. If some optimist hope of this kind was pardonable in the beginning of the former reign, now, after thirty years of experience, we may doubt the very sincerity of such a tardy hopefulness. It is far more likely to be a mere device

---

claimed he would be happy to give even 20,000. The clerk refused to give any explanation and they parted. At the next month Mr. K—— received a telegram stating: the allowance is granted by the Emperor. Full of exultation, he rushed once more to St. Petersburg, receives his 200,000, found the clerk, his benefactor, and gave him the 20,000 roubles promised. Touched by such an act of honesty and faithfulness to a promise made in a momentary excitement, the clerk said that he wanted to tranquillize the conscience of Mr. K—— by explaining to him that in obtaining the allowance no underhand means were employed, and all was done with complete honesty and fairness. He then told him the small device which was used to make the Emperor change his mind. "We have," he said, "always a great number of things to present for the Emperor's examination. And we know beforehand what he will be pleased to read and what will be unpleasant. Now all depends on the order in which such a petition as yours is placed. If before it we put four or five unpleasant things, the Emperor, when he arrives at your petition, will be in a bad humour and refuse it. If, on the contrary, we put before it one after another five things that will be agreeable to him to read, on reaching your petition he will be put in good humour and grant it at once."

Nothing more simple indeed. The fact is perfectly authentic, and would be difficult to invent.

to conceal pusillanimity of heart. The autocracy will be destroyed, there is no doubt of it, but it will be done by force. No country had ever to sustain so hard a struggle for its political liberty as the Russia of to-day. I do not speak of the unhappy social conditions and the enormous concentration of power in the hands of the Central Government. The worst is, that in other countries the struggle for liberty was over some time ago, when civilization had not not yet put at the disposal of Government the material advantages of perfected weapons and surprisingly quick communications—advantages which are all in favour of the Government and which would have rendered utterly impossible or fruitless many a brilliant insurrection, many a splendid campaign of the heroes of liberty.

But there is no obstacle which cannot be overcome by energy, spirit of sacrifice, and courage. The Russian despotism must and will be destroyed. For it is not permitted to the stupid obstinacy of one, nor to the infamous egoism of a few, to arrest the progress and light of a nation of a hundred million souls. We can only wish that the mode of execution of the unavoidable may be the less disastrous, less sanguinary, and most humane. And there is a force which can strongly contribute to this result—it is the public opinion of European countries.

VI.

Strange but quite true ; the Russian governmental circles are much more impressed by what is said about them in Europe than by the cries of all Russia, from the White Sea down to the Euxine. There are many instances of this. All Russia heard of the horrors of our political prisons and shuddered. But year after year passed, yet the Government never thought of taking any steps to ameliorate it, nor gave any sign of having a mind to do it. But some French papers began an agitation in favour of the unfortunate Hessa Helfmann, saying that the Government, after having commuted her sentence of death, killed her by slow torture in the fortress ; and the Government of the Tzar takes an unheard-of step: it allows foreign reporters to visit the prisoner in her provisory cell to show that she is alive and rebut the accusation. Thousands of complaints and remonstrances from the most respectable bodies of citizens are not honoured by an answer, and do not produce on the wooden ears of the governing class more effect than the humming of an importunate gnat. But leaders appear in the *Times*, and a correspondent telegraphs to this paper (Dec. 24, 1884), "An extremely sore feeling has lately shown itself here in the highest circles in which the English Press is accused of having lately taken to basing its opinion about Russia upon the prejudiced writings of disguised and long-expatriated Nihilists."

And to give vent to the soreness of the higher circle's feelings, their writers spread absurd libels about Nihilists.

Such instances might easily be multiplied. What is the cause of this surprising and rather incomprehensible sensitiveness? It may be urged that European public opinion has a great influence on the Russian Government, because it depends so much on foreign money markets. Yes, it is quite true; but that is not enough. The conduct of the Government in its interior policy is far more ruinous than any loss that may be inflicted on Russia from this quarter. It does not frighten it, however.

The sensitiveness of our *camarilla* to blame from the European press must have some moral cause. There must be something of the very nature of the slave in the eve-turned master of to-day. His cruelty is prompted by cowardice. Being merciless toward the feeble, he is mean and timorous before the strong, whom he is bound to recognize.

However it may be, the fact is a fact: the Russian governmental caste are extremely zealous to conceal from the public opinion of Europe their misdeeds, and very sensitive to what is said about them abroad.

But if the influence of European public opinion was limited only to vexing of the governing caste it would have been of little use indeed to appeal to it. Its influence may be exercised in a much more effective way.

It is a mistake, even nonsense, I dare say, to affirm that the Russian Government is supported by the mere physical force of its soldiers or the ignorance of its peasants. If all those who are against the existing *régime* in their heart had resolved to show it openly, the autocracy could not stand a single day. However small in numbers, the instructed classes are the moving spirits and the nerve centres of every social body. These classes are in immense majority against the existing system. There is a great deal of difference in the parties that divide it. But, besides those who do not care about anything at all, and a lot of scoundrels who profit by the existing anarchy in the administration to fill their own pockets, all the these classes are against the existing *régime*. And the reader who remembers what we have just exposed will surely find they have sufficient reasons to be so. If these classes had resolved to act boldly and energetically, without being afraid of that temporary severity the Government may inflict on them, the autocracy, decrepit and timorous as it is, odious to a great part of its own functionaries, could not stand against their common efforts. If the Press—when Russia had still a Press—had profited by the many moments of governmental panic after the Terrorists' successful attempt, had had the courage to ask energetically as one man for freedom and reform, the Government would have hesitated perhaps before suspending them all. If now all the Zemstvos made a general demand for a free constitution, the Government could not disperse them all. Such an act would have produced a more disastrous and permanent effect on the Government's funds and finances than a war.

It is on these elements of Russian society that the public opinion of free countries has—as every Russian will admit—a most decisive and beneficial influence. Every energetic manifestation of sympathy for our liberative movement from the people of the neighbouring countries is an event for Russia, and has no less a moral effect on our people than a manifestation of opposition in Russia itself. That is the mode in which European countries can contribute to strengthening the liberal movement of our country.

And no moment is more opportune for this kind of moral intervention than the present. For the Russian revolutionary movement is passing now through an important phase of its development. Having begun by terrorism, it is entering on a period which may be called insurrectional. The attempts against the functionary and the Emperor are no more its means of struggle. Having acquired great adherence in the army, and among the working classes of the capital and other principal towns, it has enlarged its aim and its prospects. It has written on its banner open though unexpected attack against the autocracy itself. Insurrections like that of the Decembrists of 1825, only more exclusively military, are now the chief object of Russian revolutionists. This is not an easy task, nor to be prepared from one fortnight to another, as an attempt against the person of an Emperor. It is a long and hard work, and many a noble victim may fall; many unsuccessful attempts may precede the definitive victory of Russian liberty. The quickness of their success depends entirely on the degree of preparation in the bulk of Russian society, in the degree of its energy at the moment of the starting of such bold attempts.

Whether the initiative of the attack on the autocracy will be made by the revolutionists, or the more moderate part of Russian society will outstrip them by pacific but energetic demonstrations, which we revolutionists will be the first to applaud—the public opinion of European countries is of great, inestimable value. And that is the reason why we appeal to it.

Addressing ourselves now to the English people, we have not the slightest doubt that such an appeal will find an echo in many thousands of English hearts. There was never a striving of any country for its liberty which found not the warmest support in England : from those of the small tribes of Candiots, to those of Hungarian, Polish, and Italian patriots. Our cause appeals no less to every generous heart. Our sufferings are something unheard-of in the bloody annals of despotism. It is not a political party, I repeat, it is a whole nation of a hundred millions that is stifled, a nation which, by the intelligence, aptitude for instruction, and kind-heartedness of its masses ; by the good and unselfish disposition of its upper classes and the generous ardour of its young generation, presents the best guarantees of a lasting progress and happy future.

Humanity is the chief, the main claim of our cause for sympathy and support. But it is not the the sole one.

It was a question of pure humanity when the Bulgarian horrors were spoken of. It was a question of humanity when Mr. Gladstone held up to public obloquy the King of Naples, nicknamed Rè Bomba, for his atrocious treatment of political prisoners.

With Russia it is no more a question of humanity only, but of general safety and common interest. However badly administered, however ruined, it is too enormous a body not to endanger by its presence other political bodies which surround it. An army of a million of soldiers, who, although dying from hunger and half clad, for courage in the field is not inferior to any other in the world. Such an enormous force left to the uncontrolled caprice of a despot or a courtier is surely a great impediment to human intercourse. To have such a State for a neighbour is nearly as unpleasant as to sit by an unfettered madman at an evening party. Nobody can answer for what he will do the very next moment. Now, when I am writing, an absurd, useless, bloody Afghan war is perhaps at hand. No Russian parliament would have answered the proposition otherwise than with laughter. It is a well-known device of despots to get rid of a burning internal question. If it pass over now, who may answer for to-morrow, when the need of such a diversion may be more stringent, or the ambition of some bloodthirsty soldier more prevailing?

Only the destruction of Russian autocracy can constitute Russia a guarantee of peace and free Europe from external danger. That is a consideration on which it is superfluous to insist.

I allow myself to point another which has not so great an interest for Englishmen, but which they will allow me to mention in few words:

In 1547 the Tzar, John IV., sent to Germany, a Saxon of the name Shlitte, ordering him to obtain for the Moscovite service artisans and scholars of every kind. Shlitte did as he was bidden, and after some time he had more than a hundred people with whom he proposed to return to Muscovy. But the magister of the Livonian order, which occupied then the Baltic province, remonstrated with the Emperor, Charles V., against the danger that might come to Livonia and neighbouring German states if the Moscovite Empire should pass from barbarity to culture. The German Emperor listened to the remonstrance, and the Livonian magister was told to stop the hundred Shlitte's men at Lubeck, and not to allow a single scholar or artisan to cross the Moscow frontier.

What in the sixteenth century the Livonian did, the German Chancellor is doing now. Russia would be too strong for him once free. And the Iron Prince is doing his best to prevent freedom crossing the Russian frontier. He needs not to appeal to any foreign power; to prevent such an annoyance, he has found the best ally in Count Tolstoi and consorts. These work for their own as well as for his interest. What the triumvirs might fail perhaps to maintain by their own exertion, they do by aid of the great personal influence and authority of the German Chancellor on the Tzar. The service is mutual. Tolstoi and company are masters of the State's cash-box. Bismarck is the master in Europe. Russia of to-day is nothing more than a Caliban, a savage and deformed slave, whom the Prussian Prospero with the three hairs on his head may use for every base work he likes. And with such a slave on his chain, what may this Prospero not venture? As long as Russia remains what she is he will be the dictator and arbiter of Europe, and so long Prussian militarism, which is the scourge of civilized Europe, will remain unchecked.

All who are for progress, for peace and humanity, should unite in a moral crusade against Russian despotism.

NOTE.—I have to offer an apology for the shortcomings of the foregoing chapter. It is the only one which I have attempted to write in English.—S. S.

THE END.

www.ingramcontent.com/pod-product-compliance
Lightning Source LLC
Chambersburg PA
CBHW032059220426
43664CB00008B/1065